Careers for You Series

CAREERS FOR

CLASS CLOWNS

& Other Engaging Types

JAN GOLDBERG

SECOND EDITION

McGraw·Hill

New York   Chicago   San Francisco   Lisbon   London   Madrid   Mexico City
Milan   New Delhi   San Juan   Seoul   Singapore   Sydney   Toronto

Library of Congress Cataloging-in-Publication Data

Goldberg, Jan
      Careers for class clowns & other engaging types / Jan Goldberg— 2nd ed.
         p.   cm. — (McGraw-Hill careers for you series)
        ISBN 0-07-143856-4 (alk. paper)
         1. Performing arts—Vocational guidance.   2. Clowning—Vocational
guidance.   3. Juggling—Vocational guidance.   4. Magicians—Vocational
guidance.   I. Title: Careers for class clowns and other engaging types.
II. Title.   III. Series.

    PN1580.G568   2005
    791'.023—dc22   2004019295

1 2 3 4 5 6 7 8 9 0   DOC/DOC   0 9 8 7 6 5

ISBN 0-07-143856-4

McGraw-Hill books are available at special quantity discounts to use as premiums and sales promotions, or for use in corporate training programs. For more information, please write to the Director of Special Sales, Professional Publishing, McGraw-Hill, Two Penn Plaza, New York, NY 10121-2298. Or contact your local bookstore.

This book is printed on acid-free paper.

This book is dedicated to the memory
of my beloved parents,
Sam and Sylvia Lefkovitz,
and to a dear aunt, Estelle Lefko.

Contents

Acknowledgments

The author gratefully acknowledges the following individuals for their contributions to this project:

- The numerous professionals who graciously agreed to be profiled in this book
- My dear husband, Larry, for his inspiration and vision
- My children, Deborah, Bruce, and Sherri, for their encouragement and love
- Family and close friends—Adrienne, Marty, Mindi, Cary, Michele, Paul, Michele, Alison, Steve, Marci, Steven, Brian, Jesse, Bertha, Uncle Bernard, and Aunt Helen—for their faith and support
- Diana Catlin, for her insights and input

The editors at McGraw-Hill also acknowledge the work of career writer Mark Rowh, who revised and updated this edition.

CHAPTER ONE

Clowning Around

An Introduction

In every group, there always seems to be someone with a knack for making other people laugh. Are you that type of person? Maybe you love attention—perhaps even crave it. Maybe other people think you are funny, too. If you like to think of yourself as entertaining, and others agree, then you may enjoy the feeling of having all eyes on you. In fact, if you haven't played the role already, chances are you would be the ideal class clown.

Different Strokes

What sets class clowns apart from other people? The old phrase, "different strokes for different folks," certainly applies to these humorous types. They may use any number of approaches, but they find themselves compelled to do one thing—make themselves the focus of attention. Those who once engaged in this behavior in the schoolroom might have incurred the teacher's wrath at times, but they were usually liked by classmates. In fact, they were often admired by their peers.

In the real world, the class-clown spirit can serve as a positive force in the choice of career for those individuals who thrive on being at the center of attention. For those who are successful in making this transition, what once resulted in a trip to the principal's office might now serve as the springboard to a career as a professional comedian or other entertainer.

Bring in the Clowns!

Laughter is a basic part of human nature. The spirit of clowning has existed for thousands and thousands of years in civilizations all over the world. Individuals who have chosen clowning and other entertainment careers have made important contributions to society. Entertainment provides outlets for all of us, allowing people relief from common stresses and giving them a chance to reenergize their efforts in their daily lives.

Clowning Through History

In some form, clowns have played a part in most cultures throughout recorded history. The Spanish explorer Cortez found them when he conquered the Aztec nation in A.D. 1520. To a great degree, they were similar to the clowns that existed in Europe at that time.

Various clown characters were a part of most Native American tribes. They often played an important social and religious role in the society at the time. Some were believed to be capable of curing diseases.

Some of the earliest ancestors of the clown were a part of ancient Greek culture. These comics were bald and padded to appear larger than normal. They usually appeared in farces and mime acts, and they parodied the actions of the more serious characters. A similar character was also a part of Roman mime. This clown wore a pointed hat and colorful robe and was often the target for all the tricks and abuse of other characters in the production.

Court Jesters

Some of the earliest comedians played the role of court jester. Throughout the Middle Ages and in the early years of the Renaissance, jesters (or fools, as they were also called) perpetuated the art of clowning in the palaces of kings and nobles. Jesters played a particularly important role in the social culture of Medieval Europe by serving as "safety valves" or a "social conscience." As they were the only ones allowed to speak out against the rulers' ideas, jesters were often catalysts for social change; they were able to wield considerable power through their wit and humor.

It was also during this time that colorful costumes associated with today's clowns had their origins. Jesters adopted a standard uniform of bright green- and saffron-colored coats, hose, and a hooded cap topped by tiny bells designed to tinkle whenever the wearer moved.

Early Clowns

While many clowns entertained at court, they were far from the only performers of this type. Many, in fact, were street performers. They were adept at a variety of skills, as is often the case with clowns today. These performers engaged in magic, contortion, juggling, acrobatics, storytelling, puppetry, tightrope walking, working with trained animals, ballad singing, clever dialogue, and other methods of entertaining.

Clowns were originally called by other names. *Zany*, *jester*, *fool*, *minstrel*, and *mime* are just some of the historical synonyms for *clown*. The English equivalent used today did not appear until the sixteenth century. *Clown* originally meant "clod" and was often used to denote a clumsy country bumpkin. These rustics were considered very funny, and comedic actors imitated their ways.

The first professional stage clowns included William Kemp and Robert Armin, both of whom were connected with Shakespeare's company of actors. Through English traveling actors of the seventeenth century, Germany was introduced to stage clowns. One popular character was Pickelherring. He and his friends wore clown costumes that remain familiar today—giant ruffs around their necks, hats, and oversized shoes.

During the same time period, the spirit of improvisation reached new heights in Europe in the form of street theatre. This gave birth to a roster of comedic characters that may still be seen today. These include Harlequin, with his popular patchwork costume, and Pierrot, one of the first clowns known to use whiteface.

The first real circus clown may have been Joseph Grimaldi, who first appeared in England in 1805. Grimaldi's clown, called Joey, specialized in the classic physical tricks, such as tumbling and slapstick beatings. (Since then, clowns have often been called Joeys.) In the 1860s a low-comedy comic with a big nose, baggy clothes, large shoes, and untidy manners appeared under the name of Auguste. He worked with a clown in whiteface and always spoiled the latter's trick by appearing at the wrong time to mess things up.

Another clown known as Grock (Adrien Wettach), a famous pantomimist in whiteface, evoked laughter in his continual struggle with inanimate objects. Chairs collapsed beneath him. When a stool was too far from a piano, he shoved the piano to the stool. His elaborate melancholy was not unlike that of Emmett Kelly, the American vagabond clown.

The Big Top

By about 1900, the smaller tents of the one-ring show had given way to the big top, and the circus enjoyed a golden age. As the large new three-ring format evolved, clowns were presented with their greatest challenge yet. Spectacular movement, bright costumes, oversized props, loud explosives, and flamboyant makeup became essential ingredients in the clown's new formula for laughs.

Clowning Today

Today, the spirit of clowning involves much more than circus clowns or street performers. Stand-up comedians, actors in television comedies, movie actors, comedy writers, and many others take comedy in any number of directions. Similarly, other types of performers use their skills to entertain audiences large and small. Building on a heritage that is centuries old, they make life a little more enjoyable for everybody else.

The Class-Clown Quiz

Are you a class clown? Take the following quiz, and you'll find out.

1. Do you enjoy being the center of attention?
2. Do you purposely do things that draw attention to you?
3. Are you most comfortable when you stand out from others?
4. Is ordinary not good enough for you?
5. Do you avoid being one of many?
6. Do you like to do your own thing?
7. Do you prefer to lead rather than to follow?
8. Do you have a facility for entertaining others?
9. Are you gregarious?
10. Are you an extrovert?
11. Do you like to entertain?
12. Do you like to make others laugh?
13. Are you creative?
14. Can you memorize things easily?
15. Are you funny?
16. Are you unafraid of being in front of a group?
17. Do you enjoy performing?
18. Do you enjoy applause?
19. Do you like to travel?
20. Do you like the idea of working nights and weekends?
21. Are you comfortable having a career that is often unpredictable?
22. Do you have a pleasing personality?
23. Are you adept at selling yourself?
24. Do you like being your own boss?
25. Do you really enjoy being with people?

If you've answered yes to many of these questions, then read on. This book focuses on a number of careers that are perfect for those who possess these qualities or tendencies.

What's in a Name?

If you are lucky enough to become famous—whether as a circus clown, nightclub comedian, or performing artist—you might want to change your name and take on a "stage name" as so many other entertainers have done before you. Interspersed throughout the book are the birth names of some well-known performers, both in comedy and in other areas of entertainment. Look for them as you read the book. (Their more well-known stage names can be found at the end of the book.) Perhaps, someday, your name will also be listed among these notable entertainers!

Here's your first birth-name challenge: David Adkins.

CHAPTER TWO

Comedians

W hy did the chewing gum cross the road? Because it was stuck to the chicken. If you can get an audience to laugh at this joke, you may have a career in comedy ahead of you!

OK, so a professional comedian needs better material than this. But the opportunities are out there for those with talent, energy, stage presence, and a lot of luck.

Certainly, everyone enjoys humor. How many times have you laughed out loud at the remarks made by a comedian? Whether performing on television or connecting with a live audience, comedians hold a special place in our society. After all, who else gets paid to make people laugh?

Of course, most of us have a sense of humor, but working as a professional comedian requires special skills, along with a great deal of hard work. Most comedians create the illusion that comedy is effortless. But the real truth is that pros in this area practice their routines over and over.

Zeroing in on What a Comedian Does

It's obvious that a comedian's job is to make people laugh. But just how they achieve this varies widely among performers. Comedians entertain people by performing monologues or skits, telling jokes, delivering comic lines, and making other efforts aimed at one result: laughter. They may sing humorous songs, perform comedic dances or walks, wear funny costumes, do impersonations, or use bodily movements and facial contortions to try to make audiences react with laughter.

Comedians who work in nightclubs are often called stand-up comedians. They entertain audiences with stories, jokes, one-liners, and impressions. In comedy clubs in large cities, they may do more than one show a night, appearing either before or after another comedian. Depending on whether they are the opening act or the main act, they perform sets of material that are anywhere from ten minutes to an hour or longer.

Stand-up comedians may work alone or in pairs. When they work in pairs, one usually takes the part of the straight man (or woman) who appears to speak in a serious manner. The other person feeds off that individual in a humorous way.

Comedians may entertain audiences in nightclubs, halls, conventions, hotel parties, indoor and outdoor festivals, private parties, theatres, and concerts. Comedy clubs provide avenues for young comics to hone their talents before live audiences.

After comedians have sharpened their acts, they may be asked to appear on a television talk show or comedy special. Some comedians perform comedy concerts that are videotaped and broadcast. If comedians become really well known, they may have a television series developed for them.

Making Things Funny

Where do comedians get their material? Most write some or all of their jokes. Many also develop material for other comedians. Typically, the humor is created and built from the people and situations around them—often ordinary, everyday items like diapers or cell phones. After the material is written, comedians usually study it, trying to absorb the content and envision how they will act it out onstage. Then they practice aloud to establish timing and rhythm. Most comics perform from memory, though a few use notes or other aids.

Many comedians critique their own performances by videotaping them and then studying them carefully. Then it is time to try a live audience, perhaps at either a dinner party or in front of a friendly crowd of family, friends, or acquaintances.

The final step for the comedian is the moment of performance. To be successful at this job, you must enjoy being the center of attention under difficult circumstances.

You must be able to recall your planned material while you are analyzing the audience's feedback and making instant adjustments to keep the laughs coming. It takes a combination of solid material and personal charm to have a winning formula for success.

A comedian develops a unique style, skill, and body of work as an entertainer. Jim Carrey, Tina Fey, Robin Williams, Will Ferrell, and Whoopi Goldberg all have very distinctive comedic styles, and they have all enjoyed great success.

SOME BASIC TYPES OF JOKES

Anecdotes
Bar jokes
Caricatures
Cruelty jokes
Exaggeration
Insults
Knock-knock jokes
Limericks
Political jokes
Profession jokes
Puns
Put-downs
Relationship jokes
Satire
Scary jokes
Sex jokes
Sports jokes
Vocabulary jokes

Performance Groups

Comedy performance groups—sometimes known as comedy troupes—develop, perform, and publicize their own material. Most of the members maintain freelance or day jobs that allow them to pursue this career. They often schedule a weekly show, bracketed around rehearsal and workshops where they critique each other's sketches and performances.

Working in a group requires good timing, diligence, and the ability to adapt to unforeseen situations, such as a blown line or cue. A troupe comedian must respond to peers' comments and take criticism well. The ability to work with others is also critical to success.

Comedy troupes are often formed in major urban centers, such as Chicago or New York. They are more common in large cities, where many actors and comedians congregate because there are greater opportunities to find work.

Getting Started in Comedy

Comedians come from all walks of life. Some hold bachelor's or graduate degrees. Others have not even graduated from high school. Although there are no formal education requirements, advanced learning is definitely a plus in this line of work. It gives you a much broader base of knowledge from which to draw humor. Course work in drama, communications, speech, theatre, English, composition, business, broadcasting, and public speaking are all advantageous (both at the high school and college levels). If you can find classes or workshops in comedy performance or writing, so much the better.

Comedians need to be able to perform a variety of tasks, must know how to deal with people, and should have a pleasant speaking voice. In addition, a successful comedian must be quick-witted, able to think on his or her feet, dedicated, and lucky. A great deal of self-confidence is needed if one is to last more than two years in this profession (and over half don't). Failure, disappointment, and rejection are common.

The Reality: Paying Your Dues

The concept of paying your dues has been a long-standing one in the comedy world. Even the most successful comedians start out modestly, in most cases. Paying your dues may mean performing in dingy nightclubs before an audience of one and walking away without a penny to show for it. Stand-up comedians have a more uncertain road than troupe comedians, going from club to club, writing material, practicing and refining it, and hoping for a break.

It is not unusual for aspiring stand-up comics to log over two hundred days per year away from home, traveling from city to city, entertaining different types of audiences, and sharpening their acts in the process. To book these out-of-town performances, the comedians may call the club owners themselves or go through a booking agent. In medium- and small-sized cities, they often perform only one night and then drive or fly to the next city.

While it can be a glamorous profession, comedy also brings many difficulties. Aside from being away from home for much of the year, comedians are also very vulnerable. Comedians go onstage alone, and if they don't make the crowd laugh, they have no one to blame but themselves. But when the audience does laugh, comedians feel richly rewarded.

Making It in the Comedy World

While it can be difficult to succeed in the entertainment business, opportunities for comedians are more common than one might realize. Of course it takes an unusual combination of skills and hard work to make it as a comedian, but the possibilities are genuine. Comedy clubs are popular in cities everywhere. There are also a large number of opportunities to appear on television, whether it be on local, network, independent, or cable station shows.

Some comedians stop working stand-up and go on to perform in situation comedies or films. The long list of performers who have successfully accomplished this includes David Spade, Jerry Seinfeld, Mike Meyers, Robin Williams, Wayne Brady, and Adam Sandler. Other comedians, such as Joan Rivers and Jay Leno, have gone on to host television talk shows.

Certainly, success takes an incredible level of perseverance. Comics must cope with rejection, criticism, and low pay while launching their careers. Comics naturally develop a style of humor that is suited to them, but finding the right niche can take years.

Competition among comedians is intense, but new opportunities are arising. Some companies, for example, now hire comedians to speak at conferences or conduct seminars for employees.

Compensation for Comedians

Working stand-up comedians may either get paid by the show or for a week of performances. The headliner makes much more than the opening act.

In large comedy clubs in the nation's major cities, a headliner can earn from $1,000 to more than $20,000 per week, depending on his or her popularity. The comedian who opens the evening's show might earn anywhere from $150 to $500 per week, while the middle comedian can earn from $500 to $1,000 per week.

At the beginning, comedians often work just to get the experience and exposure, as well as to make valuable contacts. They may also perform for "the door," which means they receive part of the admission price paid by the people who attended the show.

For comedy writers, the pay scale is also very wide. Those who write jokes for famous comedians may earn a sum such as $50 or $100 for every joke used. Those who write for television get paid different rates depending on their experience, reputation, and the budget of the show. The writers of a network comedy show can be paid anywhere from $50,000 to more than $200,000 a year.

Secrets for Success

Here are some tips for those who would like to pursue comedy as a career:

- Take classes and workshops in performing and writing comedy.
- Participate in comedy competitions, which are offered throughout the country, often sponsored by television stations, comedy clubs, or corporate sponsors. These programs are excellent ways to obtain exposure.
- Offer to emcee any type of entertainment event you can find. Consider local talent and variety shows, telethons, charity dinners, luncheons, and so forth.
- Take part in local talent and variety shows.
- Perform as often as you can to hone your skills, gain experience, and perfect your act.
- Believe in yourself! A great deal of success in this field is based upon not only talent, but drive, determination, ambition, and perseverance. Don't give up.
- Go to clubs and watch other comedians perform. Observe what makes their acts successful.
- Watch comedians who perform on television. Check out their styles, techniques, timing, and content.
- When you and your act are ready, try to get a paying job in comedy. Remember—make sure you are ready!
- Locate all nightclubs and comedy clubs in your area and find out the requirements for performing. Many have amateur or open-mike nights as well as talent showcases where new entertainers can try out material and hone their acts.
- Consider talking to local bands, singers, and other musical acts about opening for them.
- When you are ready, contact agents who specialize in booking comedy acts.

Training in Comedy

It has been said that the best place for a comedian to learn this demanding craft is in the school of hard knocks. But it is also possible to find classes and seminars on the art and craft of comedy. Such offerings are not available everywhere, but it may be worthwhile to check on their availability in your geographical area. Or, if you are serious about pursuing a comedy career, you may want to consider traveling to a location where classes are offered. Here are brief overviews of two such programs.

San Francisco Comedy College offers both introductory and advanced classes, ranging from a free introductory seminar to detailed classes covering a wide range of topics. Classes are held in four northern California locations (San Francisco, San Jose, Santa Cruz, and Sacramento), and performances take place in a wide variety of locations.

The initial workshop introduces students to a tool called the Joke Diagram, a formula that illustrates the structure of virtually all funny stories and jokes. It also includes an overview of the workshops offered through the Comedy College, tips on rehearsal techniques, and more.

The Comedy College's more advanced Working Comedians Workshop is targeted to the needs of professional comedians. It covers week-to-week management of a comedy career, chances to define goals, and comedy assignments and exercises. Participants benefit from public performances, private writing sessions, group performances, and one-on-one meetings, as well as background information on various business angles of a comedy career.

For more information on these and related classes and seminars, contact:

San Francisco Comedy College
414 Mason, #705
San Francisco, CA 94102
www.sfcomedycollege.com

In New York, the Upright Citizens Brigade Theatre (UCBT) Training Center offers the chance to study improv, or improvisational comedy. Students start at an introductory level and then proceed to more advanced concepts. Offerings include intensive, two-week summer workshops as well as classes spread out over longer time periods. In addition to learning about performing comedy, students may take sketch-writing classes that cover the basics of writing comedy for the stage and television.

Students and teachers in these programs have gone on to write, perform, or produce television shows such as "Saturday Night Live," "Late Night with Conan O'Brien," "The Daily Show with Jon Stewart," "Mad TV," and more.

For information, contact:

Upright Citizens Brigade Theatre
307 West Twenty-sixth Street
New York, NY 10011
www.ucbtheatre.com

For other training opportunities around the United States and Canada, check with comedy clubs, acting schools, or others who have show-business connections. Some classes can also be located online by searching for terms such as *comedy classes* or *classes for comedians.*

What Prospective Comedians Learn

Whether they pick up skills through formal classes or through experience, prospective comedians seek to learn about topics such as the following:

- How to identify comedic material
- What it means to be funny
- How to write jokes
- Basic types of comedy
- Improv techniques

- How to react to audiences
- Body language basics
- How to develop a stage presence
- How to build confidence
- Simple tricks of the comedy trade
- How to work with microphones
- How to work on camera
- How to work with a partner
- How to work in groups
- Business basics
- Self-promotion strategies

Words from the Pros

Introducing Randy Judkins

Before pursuing his comedy-related career, Randy Judkins received a bachelor of science degree in secondary education and mathematics at the University of Southern Maine and took some master's classes at Wesleyan University in Connecticut. He has studied acting, circus arts, and mime and has served as a part-time college professor. He now serves as an "EDUtrainer"—an inspirational speaker and performer.

Things fell into place for Randy in phases. At first, he concentrated on a one-man character comedy show. Then after about fifteen years of such work, he discovered a technique for blending interactive entertainment with research on human-resource topics such as change, team building, humor, and self-esteem.

"I actually love being onstage, making people laugh," he says. "Consequently, my mission has been to diversify enough to reach as many sectors of society as possible."

Randy says that his experiences as a member of a large family from a close-knit neighborhood contributed to a playful attitude. He has applied this outlook to his work onstage and with people in general. He also cites his experiences in performing, both as a young person and an adult, with organizations such as the Boy Scouts and the YMCA.

Randy's job has many facets to it. On one day, he may drive for several hours to put on a presentation for a group of teachers at a staff-development day. On a different day, he may hop a plane to another state to serve as a conference keynote speaker. He also spends time in his office following up on referrals, developing new clients, booking flights, and planning presentations to companies whose interests range from health care to manufacturing.

"I spend from forty to fifty hours per week doing what I love to do," he says. "Most of my clients provide me with an outstanding working atmosphere. When the environment is subpar, I can usually shift enough things around (including my own thinking) to produce a successful event."

Randy says he loves the interaction with his audiences. He often creates sketches that involve audience members on different levels.

"My advice to others would be to get out there and work, first for just the experiences and little pay. As your reputation grows, if it does (and you still love doing it), then it may be possible for you to carve out your niche, set some short- and long-term goals, and get some support for the skills you need to pull it all off. Go for it!"

Here is your next birth-name challenge: Marshall Mathers III.

For More Information

Organizations
To learn more about careers in this field, contact:

American Federation of Television and Radio Artists (AFTRA)
New York National Office
260 Madison Avenue
New York, NY 10016
www.aftra.org

American Federation of Television and Radio Artists (AFTRA)
Los Angeles National Office
5757 Wilshire Boulevard, Ninth Floor
Los Angeles, CA 90036
www.aftra.org

American Guild of Variety Artists (AGVA)
184 Fifth Avenue
New York, NY 10010

Screen Actors Guild (SAG)
360 Madison Avenue, Twelfth Floor
New York, NY 10017
or
5757 Wilshire Boulevard
Los Angeles, CA 90036
www.sag.org

Books

Brown, Judy. *The Funny Pages: 1,473 Jokes from Today's Funniest Comedians*. Andrews McMeel Publishing, 2002.

Epstein, Lawrence J. *The Haunted Smile: The Story of Jewish Comedians in America*. PublicAffairs, 2001.

Krutnik, Frank. *Hollywood Comedians: The Film Reader*. Routledge, 2003.

Ramuno, Phil; Henry Winkler; and Mary Lou Belli. *The Sitcom Career Book: Guide to the Louder, Faster, Funnier World of TV Comedy*. Backstage, 2004.

Schwensen, Dave. *How to Be a Working Comic: An Insider's Guide to a Career in Stand-Up Comedy*. Watson-Guptill Publications, 1998.

Wilde, Larry, et al. *Great Comedians Talk About Comedy*. Executive Books, 2000.

CHAPTER THREE

Enter the Clowns!

I n general, the term *clowning* (in this book and elsewhere) can refer to virtually any type of behavior that results in laughter. In that sense, Adam Sandler, Wayne Brady, and Courteney Cox, and countless other performers who grace stage and screen, are clowns. But in a stricter sense, clowns have a very specific place in the entertainment world.

A Special Role

What image comes to mind when you hear the word *clown*? Most of us think of a painted face, complete with bulbous nose and enormous lips, an image that's bound to elicit a smile.

Clowns divert and entertain audiences by performing comical routines, often while wearing unusual makeup and costumes. Actually, they are actors and comedians whose job is to make people laugh and have a good time. Often they wear outlandish costumes, paint their faces, and use a variety of performance skills to entertain audiences. To accomplish this, they may juggle, dance, walk on stilts, perform magic tricks, work creatively with balloons, make use of body antics, and employ a host of other skills.

Some clowns perform in large groups, as they do in a circus. Circus clowns often perform routines while the rings are being prepared for other acts. They might sing songs, tell jokes, or do acrobatic stunts. Some of the routines they perform are written specifically for them (or they write routines for themselves). Others are well-known comedy routines.

Clowns need a good sense of timing and balance and must be able to adjust their performances to the audience. They must have a good sense of humor, enjoy working and interacting with people, and be able to shift gears and adapt quickly to the way an audience responds to the act.

Clowns come from all walks of life, but one thing they all have in common is that they are creative people who love to entertain. In becoming clowns, they often develop a distinct stage persona for their acts or routines that reflects aspects of their personality or a personality they wish to portray.

How do you develop a clown character? Three key elements are (1) overall appearance, including costume; (2) makeup; and (3) personality. In order to correctly project their personae, the respective clown characters must wear appropriate costumes and makeup.

Clown Types

There are three basic types of clowns. Which appeals to you most?

The White-Faced Clown

Typically, the white-faced clown is the "straight" clown in skits. He or she is easily identified by the makeup, which has a base of white greasepaint. The "straight" clown is the one who acts very serious but who ends up being the brunt of the skit or the punch line. The costumes of white-faced clowns are usually more formal than those of other clowns. This means that the colors tend to match and the costume flows together. Other clown types tend to wear more gaudy or mismatched colors.

Makeup of the white-faced clown is typically simple and highlights natural features (eyes, lips, cheeks) already prominent on the face. Variations of a white-faced clown are unlimited. There are no specific guidelines except the basic white base.

The Auguste Clown

The silly clown in skits is usually the Auguste clown. Makeup for these clowns is a bright flesh-tone base. Auguste clowns usually appear to be unaware of what's going on in the skit, but somehow they manage to escape being the brunt of everything (a technique called the *blow off*). Costumes of Auguste clowns tend to be gaudy, mismatched, and very bright. Primary colors are most popular, and the clothing is usually oversized.

The makeup is also bright and exaggerates the natural features already present in the face (large nose, large mouth, and so on). Again, there are many variations, and all clowns adapt their own special features, which become their trademarks.

The Character Clown

The character clown is just what you would suspect—a character who is exaggerated into a clown. The most popular example of this is the Hobo or Tramp clown. This clown is usually seen with tattered clothes, including a worn hat, a red nose, makeup that suggests a week's worth of beard, and other exaggerated features.

Character clowns can represent almost any walk of life. Some of the other well-known examples are police officers, women, or babies.

Where to Find Clowns

You might be surprised at the variety of places where clowns work. They can be found in circuses, movies, television shows, fairs, musical plays, fairgrounds, or amusement parks. Many clowns work for commercial employers. Probably the most famous is Ronald McDonald, who is almost synonymous with McDonald's franchises. Some clowns work at rodeos, entertaining the crowd between events. Bullfighters also dress like clowns, but their job is to distract the bull when a cowboy falls off a horse.

This is serious work because dealing with huge, angry bulls is a risky business.

Other clowns are self-employed and may entertain at parties, birthday celebrations, school shows, senior-citizen events, country or state parks, trade shows, or conventions. They may work at automobile shows or shopping malls. Their job is to attract the attention of passersby and direct their attention to the event. Many clowns work an established circuit to make a living.

Shrine Clowns

Shrine Clowns typically belong to the International Shrine Clown Association. These clowns strive to cheer up children who are in Shrine hospitals, and they work in a variety of other ways to raise money for Shrine causes. As members, they receive newsletters and may attend conferences. Members report that they reap great personal rewards when engaging in the International Shrine Clown Association's efforts.

Circus Time

Circuses come in both large and small sizes. The smaller ones entertain in shopping malls, at state and county fairs, and in similar locations.

Circus people travel. They may set up their shows in fifty or sixty towns between April and October. Large circuses such as Ringling Brothers and Barnum and Bailey Circus may tour from January through November. The stay in any one place may last only a day, two or three days, or as long as five weeks. Winter quarters are often in Florida and California, but they can also be found in Texas, Missouri, Oklahoma, or New Jersey.

At one time, circuses traveled by train and used horse-drawn wagons to parade through towns and set up the big top. Then trucks began to move equipment around the circuit. Today, it is more common for compact truck and bus convoys to carry equipment, performers, and animals. Performers may travel in their own air-conditioned motor homes. Some circus people stay at motels or hotels when they perform in one place for several days. At every town, a circus staff member picks up and distributes personal mail to the performers.

Generally, large circuses perform indoors in stadiums, arenas, and large halls. Some small ones, however, still play under canvas tents. No two places are the same, and each stop presents special restrictions. The circus must obey local safety and health laws. Many towns insist on inspections and permits before they let the circus perform. While the arena may be large and comfortable in one city, the next city's circus site may be smaller or a more difficult place in which to perform.

Circus performers on the road have few free hours. Although their acts take only a short time, they give two shows a day, and sometimes three, afternoons and evenings, Sundays and holidays. They must also rehearse between shows. A flawless performance and perfect timing come only after years of hard work and a great deal of practice.

Performers take care of their costumes, set up and take down equipment, put on makeup, and handle other tasks related to the performance, and they may have other assigned tasks. Their time is seldom their own.

Clowns in the Spotlight

With their comic antics, the clowns relieve the tension of dangerous acts. Many clowns are physical performers. They may ride horseback or do tightwire acts. Some are jugglers, acrobats, or musicians.

When the ring conductor blows the whistle to signal the start of a show, all entertainers and animals join the opening parade around the arena track. A circus performance consists of three to four dozen acts. The band conductor and musicians play the music for each act. All acts are timed, and acts under way in all three rings finish at the same time.

Becoming a Clown

The road to clowning varies from one performer to another. Like other actors, clowns benefit from a solid education. A high school diploma is not required by most circuses, but a diploma and a college education certainly help a clown's job prospects. Employers in the motion picture and television industry also prefer to hire performers who have diplomas.

While attending high school or college—or at any time—it's a good idea to develop some basic performing skills. Many high schools offer drama or dance classes for students. Shows are put on regularly by high schools and community centers. Experience in acting or performing in plays is very helpful. Dance academies, schools for dramatic arts, and colleges and universities offer classes in pantomime and dance. Clowns need to move well and be able to use their bodies to communicate. Training in magic, juggling, acrobatics, clown makeup, costuming, choreography, and the history of clowning can also be helpful.

Some clowns also need to learn to project their voices. Debate or public-speaking clubs or classes can help to develop this ability.

Every trip, fall, and stumble that a clown takes on the arena floor has been intricately choreographed long beforehand and is the result of months, even years, of intensive training. In developing the skills of their profession, clowns learn to perform somersaults, backflips, and tumbling runs. They may learn to launch themselves over a specialized vaulting horse in any number of comedic positions or undertake other types of acrobatic falls. The next time you see a bumbling, stumbling clown tumbling into a heap, remember you're watching a trained professional in action!

There are a number of classes and programs that you can attend around the country to learn the rudimentary skills of clowning or to advance your existing knowledge. Mooseburger Camp is a five-day annual camp that offers classes such as The Business of Birthday Parties, Circus and Stage-Show Skits, Clowning 101, Comic

Movement and Mime Skills, and Prop Building. Various clown associations and organizations also hold seminars and conventions where there may be educational opportunities.

Clown Compensation

Although there are no set salaries for clowns, the following represents average salaries. Remember, however, that clowns usually do not receive paid vacations or retirement benefits.

- Birthday parties—$50 to $250 for a thirty- to ninety-minute show
- Festivals or rodeos—$100 to $300 per engagement
- Circus acts—$200 to $600 weekly (may also receive room and board)
- TV or film—$300 to $1,500 average weekly income during peak season

From a numbers viewpoint, the outlook for people who want to work as clowns is not very promising. There is a tremendous amount of competition, and the field is overcrowded, as are other segments of the entertainment industry. Wages may be controlled by unions. Like most performing artists, most clowns are not permanently employed and must repeatedly audition for positions. Too, clowns often don't receive the proper recognition for their work.

Getting Started in Clowning

If you want to become a clown, one way to get started is to find a circus and ask the manager for any work available. Often the circus needs workers to sell tickets and refreshments or to water and exercise the animals.

Some performers have a booking agent or personal manager. Others put ads in trade magazines or on websites. Performers who have a good act might ask the directors or managers of state and county fairs, television shows, and nightclubs for an audition. Performers not yet established may find work at carnivals, amusement parks, ocean piers, rodeos, ice and water shows, and other places that draw spectators.

Some modern-day clowns run small businesses out of their homes, typically on a part-time basis. They perform for children's birthday parties, school events, or other activities.

Words from the Pros

Introducing Charlie the Clown

Charlie Stron, also known as Charlie the Clown, is an entertainer based in Las Vegas, Nevada.

"I always considered myself to be shy," he says. "I never thought I would be so comfortable in front of crowds."

During high school in South Africa, Charlie used to go to a children's youth circus group that practiced all kinds of entertainment seen in circuses. He emulated what he saw and found that he had a natural ability to juggle and balance. While playing in this way, he developed circus-type skills and found himself enjoying the attention that he gained by doing the things he had learned.

After high school he was drafted into the South African army, and after basic training he was transferred into the Entertainment Unit. This experience in the army led him into the professional circus circuit in Europe, where he worked with a flying trapeze act called the Star Lords. Then he did a juggling act. Eventually he ended up in the United States, working for Disneyland with Ringling Brothers Circus. He also worked as a Clown College instructor for Ringling Brothers Clown College before he moved to Las Vegas.

"I love my job," Charlie says. "Not that it isn't difficult some-times. Don't underestimate what is involved. Still, I wouldn't trade it for anything in the world. When I'm on the road, I entertain at different kinds of fairs. Part of my act consists of four one-hour shifts on stilts using different costumes. I meet and greet thousands of people, pose in pictures, make balloon animals, and juggle on the stilts. You could consider it dangerous, but—knock on wood—I have never fallen. It is a lot safer than the trapeze act I did before and pays a lot better. "

For Charlie, one of the best things about working as an entertainer is the chance to meet all kinds of other entertainers at different events. He especially enjoys meeting old friends a few years down the road when they work together again.

"To be successful as a clown, you have to love people and be able to keep a big smile on your face," he says. "Remember, you should be a nice guy or lady by nature and not by demand. When it really comes down to it, you've got to entertain from your heart."

Introducing Gumdrop the Clown

Melo Dee Pisha, also known as Gumdrop the Clown, attended a traditional college and then went on to a succession of clown sites, including Clown Camp at the University of Wisconsin, Mooseburger University at the University of Minnesota, and clown conventions and workshops in the United States and England.

She also sought instruction as an actor-director and trained others in theatre and clown skills in local schools and park districts. She has performed in plays such as *Charlie and the Chocolate Factory*. Her challenges have included casts of up to fifty children, ages eight through eighteen.

Her career got its start when she answered an ad in the Worcester, Massachusetts, newspaper looking for someone who was willing to learn clowning and to assist another clown. Since she had a theatre background and was looking for something fun to do, she decided to give it a try.

"I had always loved to be funny," she says. "In high school I would dress up as Harpo Marx (with a few friends filling out the Marx brothers' team) and entertain at basketball games. When I started clowning, it was as if a whole new world opened up to me. I was center stage! The audience loved me. And I loved being able to make people so happy, to help them forget their worries for a few minutes."

At first Melo worked as a clown about four or five times a month, but after more training, she says she fell in love with everything about being a clown and actively marketed herself so that she could work more often.

"On a typical clown day, I spend about an hour putting in my contacts, slapping on the greasepaint, combing my wig, and getting dressed," she says. "I have different bags or suitcases for each event I am doing that day. So I make sure each one is packed appropriately for the job with the right magic tricks, balloons, or face paints. Sometimes I don't carry any props or balloons and just clown! In any case, whatever I wish to take with me that day (including a sound system, if needed) gets loaded into the van, and I'm off!"

Melo notes that as a clown, she has to be 'on' whenever she is exposed to the public. Since she is not following a script, she must think constantly about upcoming actions and dialogue.

After all is done and it is time to go home and take off her clown costume, she says she is very tired and limp. But she enjoys most clown moments.

"I love the expression on people's faces when they are having fun and are really into what I'm doing," she says. "Also, clowning has opened up many doors to me personally that I am sure I wouldn't have experienced otherwise. This includes being able to throw out the first pitch for our local baseball team and being part of a parade in Disney World! I have also formed many dear friendships with other clowns, which helps to keep up my desire to continue."

On the downside, she sometimes gets the impression that some people think what she does is unimportant or isn't a real job.

"They still think of professional clowning as a hobby or something you might do for Halloween," she says. "Clowns spend many hours on preparation, and like other professions, we have to keep attending classes and workshops to learn new and ever-better techniques. We are usually very skilled—not just in the technical clown skills, but also in child behavior, marketing, and management."

Melo advises others interested in entering this field to first contact a professional clown. If that is not possible, she feels it is wise to check out clown organizations (see the list at the end of this chapter).

Introducing Mama Clown and Friends

Mama Clown heads Mama Clown and Friends, a full-service company that plans parties and events and provides entertainment. Mama Clown, also known as Marcella Murad, attended Broward Community College for two years, then attended Clown Camp at the University of Wisconsin. She also has completed advanced studies in the art of clowning and attended Laughmakers Conferences and numerous conventions and seminars. She has earned several awards for her work.

"To live my life performing as a clown is not something that I planned," she says. "It happened little by little as I learned to love what I do with all my heart. It didn't take long to realize how lucky I am to have found a career that pays me to act like a child, make a difference in a child's life, and lift people's spirits. I have always been an easygoing person with a good sense of humor. Clowning came very naturally to me, and in my years of clowning, not once have I wished to be doing something else."

She says she enjoys all aspects of her job. That includes performing, writing articles for clown magazines or books on the subject, creating new products, and serving as an instructor.

A typical weekday for Marcella starts at 7:00 A.M. with breakfast and a visit to the gym. Then she takes care of tasks such as taking mail orders to the post office, writing a new show, preparing for a show, or actually performing a show. On a typical weekend, she entertains at an average of four events a day. This is exhausting because it takes so much energy, but it is extremely rewarding to be part of all the celebrations.

"What I love the most about my job are the smiles and friendliness that my character brings out in children of all ages," she says. "I love my work because it is so much fun, and it keeps me young at heart. There aren't many downfalls, except maybe the few times when I encounter rude people or when I see children in pain."

She advises others to make sure they genuinely like children. "Children have a sixth sense and can tell if you are sincere," she says. "They will react to you according to the vibes they sense coming from you."

She adds that if you truly love what you do, success will follow. It is not easy becoming a performer, she points out, and a great deal of dedication is needed to achieve your goals.

"Many people think that to be a clown all you need are baggy clothes, a big pair of shoes, some makeup, and a business card," Marcella says. "Nothing can be further from the truth. Clowning is an art that takes a lifetime to master. Being funny is a serious business, and becoming a professional involves a large investment of your time and money."

Introducing Soda Pop the Clown

Rick Struve, also known as Soda Pop, is based in Iowa. After graduating from high school, he went to college for about two years, focusing on liberal arts and art. He attended four years of Clown Camp in Wisconsin, but the majority of his actual clown training has come about through books and old-fashioned experience. He also continues to learn through clown friends when they get together and share information.

His specialties are magic, juggling, balloons, and face painting. He performs at events ranging from birthday parties and company picnics to city festivals. He also runs a clown website and produces an online clown newsletter.

Rick recalls that he has always fooled around with magic, but he started reading more and more about it as he grew older. He started juggling, and then he met someone who thought that he would make a good clown and pointed him in the direction of Clown Camp. He performed his first show the weekend after he returned from camp, and he hasn't stopped since.

"In a way, clowning is fairly unique when it comes to prior experience," he says, "because you don't need any! Obviously, there are classes, books, and videos to make you a better clown, but it is all based on you. Clowning is truly in the heart—corny, but very true. Very few special people can be successful at professional clowning. Necessary talents include people skills, patience, love of children, and overcoming the fear of being in front of hundreds of people!"

Rick says that one benefit of being a professional clown is that he can be his own boss. The work might include tasks such as advertising, booking shows, and paying the bills, as well as going out to do the job.

A normal show includes about six magic routines, one interactive song, a juggling routine, and then balloons for all the children. Sometimes he applies face paints to the children's faces. For larger shows he might produce a live rabbit and let the children pet it afterward.

"The best part of my job is when I get in front of the audience, and all attention is on me—people are depending on me to make them smile," he says. "I love performing. The downside of clowning for me is the time it takes to get ready for a show. Standing in front of a mirror for forty-five minutes to put on makeup and then another fifteen minutes taking it off afterward can get very tiring."

Rick advises anyone thinking about clowning to begin by reading books about performing and other related skills.

"Clowning has so many different aspects to it, it is very much up to the individual," he says. "If you like magic, learn as much as you can. If you like juggling, dancing, singing, puppets, or balloons—anything—read up on the topic and make yourself stand out from others. I always find quality clown training extremely helpful, but the best training is to actually put your ideas in front of an audience. You will quickly learn what works for you and what does not. Try to watch other clowns whenever possible—they are all different. You can pick up so much from each one. But never copy them. Just learn to be the best clown you can be."

Introducing Shadow the Clown

Shadow the Clown, also known as Kathy Lange, earned a bachelor of arts in education at Central Washington University. Her major was elementary education with emphasis in early childhood education. Combining a love for children with clowning, she took Fundamentals of Clowning at Bellevue Community College in Bellevue, Washington; attended Clown Camp at Medicine Hat in Alberta, Canada; and participated in the Northwest Festival of Clowns, held in various locations in the Pacific Northwest in September of each year. She also tries to attend local workshops and conventions each year to gain new knowledge and skills.

"Most people who know me aren't all that surprised that I now put on makeup to be a clown," says Shadow. "I have always been one to be a bit goofy at times."

She says she has always loved working with children. Her first job out of college was with a gymnastics facility, working with children in a noncompetitive atmosphere. The program was designed to provide skills not just for gymnastics but for fitness, exercise, and self-esteem. A great deal of music was used, and she often dressed up in silly costumes during theme weeks.

When she left her gymnastics job after four years, she needed an outlet to be creative and still work with young children, so she took a class in clowning. The result was the birth of her clown identity, Shadow.

"Being a clown gives me, as an adult, the freedom to walk and talk silly—to make people laugh just by dressing up and making funny faces," Kathy says. "It allows me to make a child who might be going through troubled times smile and forget, even for just a few moments, the pain and despair of his or her condition. It might allow me to be remembered from a hospital visit, a parade, or any other venue I might be doing."

Kathy is not a full-time clown; she also has a day job. She feels this is the best way to operate so that she does not have to rely on clowning as her sole source of income. This approach helps her avoid stress and maintain variety in her life.

A typical Saturday in the busy season (spring and summer) may include a parade and a birthday party. The latter may include a whole new set of props and tricks.

"The atmosphere in clowning is what you make it, and it also really depends on the type of gig you are doing," she says. "A parade is relaxed and fast paced as you are moving down the route and doing the same trick over and over to a constantly changing audience. A birthday party can be relaxed or pretty crazy, depending on the age and manners of the party attendees. A company picnic, which I love to do a lot in the summer, is usually relaxed and steady moving."

Kathy says she loves the camaraderie with the children involved in her work. She also enjoys the creativity it takes to be a clown—the constant change in finding things that are new—and the ability to put a smile on a face.

"In a hospital setting, the ability to make a child who may be hurting forget for just a few minutes and smile is very rewarding," she says. "I also enjoy the crazy look you see on people's faces when you tell them you are a clown, usually an instant smile and maybe a little envy that they wish they had the personality to be a clown. I love the pure fun of it, to be totally uninhibited, in a good way, when in makeup. Society places constraints on people as we grow up, and being a clown is a vehicle to still act like a child but avoid being ridiculed for not acting your age!"

For others considering clowning, Kathy says, "Go for it! Look around in your local area for classes, attend workshops, go to Clown Camp, learn, learn, learn. Don't think makeup and a costume are the only things you need. You need skills, patience, a love for entertaining, and a love for children. Make sure your clown face is inviting and your costume is neat and colorful. Once you get started, always look to improve. Make things fresh for you and the people you are entertaining. Don't just do it for the money— visit hospitals, nursing homes, retirement centers. The people who reside there especially need cheering up with a little entertainment to break up the day, and it can be a great pick-me-up for you, too. Laughter is the best medicine. Just have fun!"

Here's another birth name challenge: Dwayne Johnson.

For More Information

The International Clown Hall of Fame and Research Center is dedicated to the preservation and advancement of clown art. Represented by professional and amateur clown associations, it pays tribute to outstanding clown performers, operates a living museum of clowning with resident clown performers, conducts special events, and maintains a national archive of clown artifacts and history. More information is available from:

International Clown Hall of Fame and Research Center
161 West Wisconsin Avenue, Suite LL 700
Milwaukee, WI 53203
www.theclownmuseum.org

Clowns of America International (COAI) is a great resource for learning about becoming a clown and other aspects of clowning. Informative articles regarding makeup, costuming, props, skit development, and so forth are provided through the official publication, called *The New Calliope*, which is published six times a year. Membership in the organization includes a spring international convention and other benefits. Membership is open to individuals sixteen and older. More information can be obtained from:

Clowns of America International (COAI)
PO Box C
Richeyville, PA 15358
www.clownsofamerica.org

Additional organizations that have information to offer about a career as a professional clown include the following:

American Guild of Variety Artists (AGVA)
184 Fifth Avenue, Sixth Floor
New York, NY 10010

Associated Actors and Artists of America
Actors' Equity Association
165 West Forty-sixth Street
New York, NY 10036
www.actorsequity.org

International Jugglers' Association (IJA)
PO Box 112550
Carrollton, TX 75011
www.juggle.org

International Shrine Clown Association (ISCA)
1723 North Cherry Street
Galesburg, IL 61401
www.shrineclowns.com

World Clown Association
PO Box 77236
Corona, CA 92877
www.worldclownassociation.com

CHAPTER FOUR

Magicians

A t one time or another, everyone has been awed by the clever performance of a magician. For a few very talented and lucky people, a career in magic has led to fame and fortune. For example, do you know who this is describing?

1. Birth name: David Seth Kotkin.
2. Birth date: September 16, 1956.
3. He gave his first magic show at the age of ten.
4. He was the youngest-ever member of the Society of American Magicians at age twelve.
5. Before leaving high school, he taught a few classes of magic to drama students at New York University.
6. He was cast as the lead in *The Magic Man*, the longest-running musical in Chicago history.
7. He is a world-renowned multimillionaire.

If you guessed David Copperfield, you're right! Of course, not everyone will be as successful as this famous performer, but many are content to enjoy a measure of success as professional magicians.

Zeroing in on What a Magician Does

Magicians don't really makes things disappear, but they make it seem that way. Performing carefully designed tricks of illusion and sleight of hand, they use their creative powers and a variety of props to entertain and mystify audiences.

Magicians are masters of illusion. They do one thing, while an audience sees another. Through a combination of complicated techniques and persuasive comments, a magician can appear to pull a rabbit out of a hat, make a handkerchief disappear, or perform other "amazing" tricks.

A magician may include a participant from the audience and secretly remove the person's wallet while a delighted audience looks on. Or a magician may use a wooden box or other prop to appear to saw a trained assistant in half.

Magicians generally depend on props such as illusion boxes, cards, or coins. Although many magicians perform similar tricks, each magician brings a unique style to his or her performance. It takes a high degree of skill to perform the different illusions. The more skilled and experienced the magician, the more complicated the illusions.

Can You Do This?

Here are some of the tricks performed by magicians:

- **Sleight of hand** (making the hand appear faster than the eye). Examples include card tricks, disappearing balls, or handkerchief tricks.
- **Illusions** (visual deceptions that may involve large objects and/or the use of special equipment). Some examples include sawing a woman in half or making an animal disappear.
- **Mentalist tricks** (appearing to read people's minds or predict the future). Examples include "guessing" people's birthdays or revealing secrets of audience members.
- **Great escapes** (escapes from seemingly impossible situations). Examples include shucking handcuffs or escaping from a cage or locked crate.

The Magician's Job

A typical performance for a magician takes place indoors in front of a live audience. There may be a crowd in a large theatre, or the audience might consist of just a few people at a birthday party. Magicians often work alone, but it is common for a magician to have one or two assistants to help during a performance. At times, a magician may have to move heavy props, such as tables or large boxes.

Developing the Magic Touch

Magicians are skilled entertainers. It can take years of practice and training to become an accomplished magician, yet it is often possible to learn some of the more basic tricks in just a short time.

Professional magicians rarely reveal in public how they performed their tricks. The reasons are obvious. If everyone knew how a trick were done, it would no longer be a trick. The element of surprise and wonder would be gone. For this reason, the most common form of training is for a budding magician to study under a professional magician. In this way, neophyte magicians learn how to perform the various illusions. Many beginning magicians start their careers working as assistants for more experienced magicians.

If possible, talk to several magicians who live in your area to find out how they feel about their work. It's also worthwhile to read magazines and books that explain some of the basic magic tricks. Try performing them in front of your family and friends. Then prepare a performance for a school or other group and see how you feel about doing this on a regular basis.

People generally do not take college or high school courses to learn magic tricks, although courses in acting or public speaking can help a magician become more effective. It is important for a magician to have good business skills, since magicians usually handle their own financial matters. It is also important for magicians to have strong sales skills, since they are always, in effect, selling themselves and their abilities to prospective clients.

A good magician is an actor who is able to deceive people without making them feel silly or embarrassed. It is important for a magician to be comfortable performing in front of large groups of people. It's also essential to be creative in developing original forms of presentation.

Training Opportunities

As noted, magic is not an academic subject traditionally taught in schools or colleges. Nevertheless, some training opportunities are available to those willing to seek them out.

A number of magicians offer lessons or classes on a local basis; consult a phone directory of your local chamber of commerce to find them. If such opportunities are not available in your area, you can locate videos, DVDs or other training materials online. For example, MagicTricks.Com (www.magictricks.com), which bills itself as the largest online professional magic shop, offers more than thirty-five hundred pages of free information about the art of magic, as well as books, videos, and other items that may be purchased. In addition, it provides links to other sites of interest, including some offering lessons or training materials.

In pursuing these or other links, keep in mind that just as in other areas, quality and reliability may vary widely if you go shopping online for magic courses or related items. Be sure to check out any provider's track record before investing your time and money.

The Financial Angle

While world-famous magicians such as David Copperfield can earn many thousands of dollars for each performance, most magicians do not earn enough from their performances to support themselves financially. The vast majority of magicians are those who perform at night or on weekends and have other full- or part-time jobs. A magician may earn anywhere from fifty dollars for performing at a birthday party to several thousand dollars for performing at a business meeting or magic show.

Like other performance artists, magicians face an uncertain employment picture. Highly skilled magicians should find many job opportunities, while those just beginning may find it difficult to secure employment. There has been a trend for some businesses to hire magicians at trade shows and sales meetings to improve interest in a product. This should create some well-paying opportunities for those with skill and a good reputation.

SOME FAMOUS MAGICIANS PAST AND PRESENT

THEN:	NOW:
Harry Houdini	David Blaine
Harry Blackstone	Lance Burton
Howard Thurston	David Copperfield
Harry Kellar	Siegfried & Roy

Words from the Pros

Introducing Carl Andrews Jr.

Carl Andrews Jr. is a comedy sleight-of-hand expert who lives and works in Florida. He has performed on Japanese television and has appeared in Las Vegas, Atlantic City, and the prestigious Magic Castle in Hollywood.

Playing the guitar in high school bands was his official introduction to show business, and he credits his success with magic to years and years of practicing and reading widely about his craft. He feels that his fascination with magic is something that everyone experiences at one time or another.

Carl's usual daily routine starts out with business, such as phone calls, e-mail, and mailings. Then he rehearses new routines and reads or studies videotapes. He performs in the evenings.

"What I like most is working for myself and doing what I enjoy for a living," he says, "which is making people laugh. I love to entertain. The only downsides would be when business is slow and being self-employed means no paid vacations."

Carl advises others who are interested in magic to study and read all they can about the field. "Develop your own unique performing character and style," he says. "Then practice, practice, practice!"

Introducing Larry Moss

Larry Moss runs an entertainment business in Rochester, New York, called Fooled Ya. He earned both a bachelor of arts degree in math and computer science and a master of science in elementary education from the University of Rochester, but he says he has no formal training in the three things he teaches and performs: magic, juggling, and balloon art. He also wrote a book on balloon sculpting that has been distributed all over the world, and he maintains a website that offers a collection of resources for balloon artists.

Before becoming interested in magic, Larry focused on music. He started playing the violin at five years old and continued through high school. He had intended to continue pursuing music, but he got sidetracked when putting together a wizard costume for Halloween one year.

"Being a performer, I went a little overboard learning to play the part of a wizard," he recalls. "I discovered that magic was a wide-open field for creative expression that I enjoyed even more than playing the violin."

Moss says that it was actually an accident that he ended up going into entertaining full-time. Making people laugh had always been important to him, but it wasn't something he expected to do for a living. He paid his way through college by performing on street corners and at birthday parties. But when he took a "real job," he decided it wasn't right for him. So he went back to school, once again paying for his education by performing. It was only when he finished school the second time that he realized what he enjoyed most was entertaining. He also came to realize that if he could finance his education by performing, he could continue to be successful in this area.

"I watch all the performers I can, all the time," he says. "I don't care if they're in my field or not. I've been influenced heavily by people doing things as diverse as clowning or ballet.

"I don't have a 'typical' day. I suppose the largest portion of my time is spent being a salesman. I sell myself and my art all day long, everywhere I go. It's not an imposing sort of selling. Mostly, I'm just being myself. I'm always 'on' and always ready to talk about my business if the opportunity arises."

Larry divides much of his time into writing about what he does, rehearsing for shows, creating new routines, and simply playing with balloons, which combines relaxing, practicing, and being creative.

"The best part about this kind of work is that I rarely see people who aren't happy," he says. "If they aren't in a great mood when I arrive, they almost always are when I leave. I get paid to make people happy. What could be more fun than that?"

On the downside, he tends to work different schedules than his friends. Another reality is that work, and therefore income, can be inconsistent.

"An entertainer makes a career by being different from others," Moss says. "Everyone looking to get into entertainment has to find their own differences and work on those above all else. Classical training can only go so far. If you only have the same skills as others around you, you can easily be replaced. But if you're unique, you'll always be needed by someone."

Introducing Bill Palmer

Bill Palmer earned a bachelor of arts degree in Germanics from Rice University in Houston and also studied music at the University of Houston for three years, but he credits his success as a magician to on-the-job training and "plenty of seminars." He comes from a family of entertainers; his father was a music educator and concert artist, so he got started when he was just a child. He saw Harry Blackstone Sr. perform his vanishing-birdcage trick in a live show and said to himself, "That's what I want to do when I grow up!" Besides performing his magic shows, he has also played in several bands.

Bill works from his home. Since his work is seasonal, during the off-season he finds alternate ways to occupy his time, such as writing and building magic props and banjos.

"I like the accolades I receive when I do a good show," he says. "I'm an applause junkie. But I dislike the grunt work—packing and setting up. The upside of being a magician is that there are people I have entertained for three generations now. But the downside is the same—there are people I have entertained for three generations now!"

To anyone wanting to follow in his footsteps, Bill advises focusing on the basics. "Don't take up entertaining unless you are willing to learn your craft from the ground up," he says. "Learn the fundamentals, then expand on them. Study with the best. Take drama courses. Learn to read and speak well. Be yourself. And take vitamins!"

Here is your next birth name challenge: Terry Jean Bollette.

For More Information

Magic Organizations

The International Brotherhood of Magicians (IBM), founded in 1922, is the world's largest organization for magicians. The organization boasts a membership of more than fifteen thousand members worldwide. It sponsors over three hundred regional organizations called Rings around the world. The International Brotherhood of Magicians is a respected organization for amateur as well as professional magicians. For more information, contact:

International Brotherhood of Magicians (IBM)
11155 South Towne Square, Suite C
St. Louis, MO 63123
www.magician.org

The Society of American Magicians (SAM) was formed in 1902 and is the oldest active organization for magic anywhere. It has more than 250 chapters around the world, and more than three hundred thousand individuals have held membership in the Society. The organization's magazine is called *M-U-M* after its motto, Magic-Unity-Might. SAM actively promotes magic as an entertainment and art form and has the world's largest youth program for magic, called the Society of Young Magicians (SYM). Young people between the ages of seven and fifteen may join SYM.
For more information, contact:

Society of American Magicians (SAM)
PO Box 510260
St. Louis, MO 63151
www.magicsam.com

Society of Young Magicians (SYM)
329 West 1750 North
Orem, UT 84057
www.tophatprod.com/sym

Another organization that focuses on young magicians is Magical Youth International. You can obtain more information from:

Magical Youth International
159 Ralston Avenue
Kenmore, NY 14217
www.magicyouth.com

A more narrow focus is taken by the Fellowship of Christian Magicians, a religious organization dedicated to the use of visual illustrations to illustrate religious presentations. Members use techniques such as sleight of hand, optical illusion, ventriloquism, puppets, balloons, clowning, juggling, and storytelling in performing for church groups or other audiences. The group publishes *The Christian Conjurer* magazine, holds conferences and workshops, and provides networking opportunities.

More details are available by contacting the organization as follows:

Fellowship of Christian Magicians
FCM Mail Center
7739 Everest Court North
Maple Grove, MN 55311
www.gospelcom.net/fcm

Magazines

A great way to keep up with modern magic is to consult one of the magazines specializing in magic-related information. *Genii*, which describes itself as the conjuror's magazine, offers a wealth of information in every issue. You can find historical articles on great magicians and their techniques, tips on how to perform specific magic tricks, updates on happenings in the world of magic, and more. Its online version also includes a forum where those interested in magic can participate in online discussions.

For information, contact:

Genii: The Conjuror's Magazine
4200 Wisconsin Avenue NW, Suite 106–384
Washington, DC 20016
www.geniimagazine.com

Another publication, *Magic: The Magazine for Magicians*, also provides readers with a wide variety of magic-related information. This monthly magazine offers profiles of working magicians, historical stories, predictions for the future, and reports on all types of magic shows. Readers can also check the "great new tricks" section each month, which offers advice from some of the world's most successful magicians.

You can also find listings of current magic performances in nightclubs, amusement parks, resorts, cruise ships, and elsewhere, as well as news, editorials, and product reviews.

For more information, contact:

Magic: The Magazine for Magicians
6220 Stevenson Way
Las Vegas, NV 89120
www.magicmagazine.com

Books

Allen, Jon. *Simple Magic Tricks: Easy-to-Learn Magic Tricks with Everyday Objects.* Hamlyn, 2004.
Eldin, Peter, and Eve Devereux. *Card & Magic Tricks.* Gramercy, 2004.

Garenne, Henri. *The Art of Modern Conjuring: For Wizards of All Ages*. Gramercy, 2004.

Hugard, Jean, and Frederick Braue. *The Royal Road to Card Magic (Cards, Coins, and Other Magic)*. Dover Publications, 1999.

King, Mac, and Mark Levy. *Tricks with Your Head: Hilarious Magic Tricks and Stunts to Disgust and Delight*. Three Rivers Press, 2002.

McEvoy, Harry K. *Knife Throwing: A Practical Guide*. Tuttle Publishing, 2004.

Scarne, John. *Scarne's Magic Tricks (Cards, Coins, and Other Magic)*. Dover Publications, 2003.

Silverman, Kenneth. *Houdini!!!: The Career of Ehrich Weiss*. Perennial, 1997.

Tyson, Donald. *The Magician's Workbook: Practicing the Rituals of the Western Tradition*. Llewellyn Publications, 2001.

Wilson, Mark. *Mark Wilson's Cyclopedia of Magic: A Complete Course*. Running Press, 1995.

CHAPTER FIVE

Jugglers and More

Those who fit into the category of "class clown" include all types. For some, being at the center of attention does not necessarily involve humor. Instead, they might offer excitement or some other brand of entertainment instead of, or in combination with, comedy. Such is the case for jugglers, who occupy a unique niche in the world of performance arts.

Jugglers are generally considered variety performers. This group also includes mimes, impersonators, ventriloquists, puppeteers, and storytellers, among others.

Jugglers may entertain audiences by working alone or in groups. They may present their acts in many ways and styles in order to meet the interests and tastes of their audiences. Performers might do a single show, or they may present a complete show in nightclubs, circuses, fairs, carnivals, motion pictures, or on television.

OBJECTS YOU CAN JUGGLE
Golf balls
Baseballs
Softballs
Glow-in-the-dark balls
Apples
Oranges
Beanbags
Clubs
Juggling sticks
Rings

Torches
Knives (handle with care!)

The Life of a Juggler

The juggler's life is not for everyone. Those comfortable with the nine-to-five world may find it too unstructured for their tastes. But for prospective entertainers, juggling can offer an interesting array of challenges and opportunities.

Jugglers perform under all kinds of conditions. They may work indoors or outdoors, at night or in the daytime. They might perform in a theatre, in a school auditorium, at a mall, or in the parking lot of a shopping center.

Nightclubs are often crowded and noisy. Studios may be hot and poorly ventilated. Gymnasiums may have no stage or poor sound systems. Conventions and trade shows can be noisy and distracting. Entertainers must be able to adjust to whatever situation is at hand.

Jugglers usually find it necessary to travel to be successful. Many such entertainers travel an established circuit. They wedge rest and meals between travel and performances. When they are first starting, most performers have little time and limited money for meals and hotel rooms.

Few entertainers of this type work regular hours. A performance may be anything from a ten-second television commercial to a full-length performance lasting several hours. They may contract for a single appearance or for a long engagement of several weeks. Besides performing, they spend a great deal of time in practice and rehearsals. A one-hour television show, for example, may require five days of rehearsal.

Keys to Success

What does it take to be a successful juggler? First, of course, is the basic skill of the juggling act itself. Typically, this is mastered first on a small scale and then polished into something that audiences will find impressive. To get to that level, jugglers need talent, stage presence, and self-confidence in order to establish a rapport with the audience. Stamina, self-discipline, commitment, and the determination to keep trying are also vital. So are strength, endurance, flexibility, coordination, and dexterity.

Since jugglers and other variety performers must sell themselves to agents, employers, and their audiences, they must have charm, style, and originality. They must also be able to work well with other performers, technicians, directors, and others. They also should be able to adapt to a constantly changing schedule as well as the stress of a scarcity of bookings.

Learning the Craft

Want to earn a bachelor's degree in juggling? Think again. There are no defined educational requirements for jugglers or other variety performers. However, a good academic background will be helpful in many aspects of this career. High school subjects should include English, the arts, and business courses. A college degree is always a strong asset. Many colleges offer programs in drama or theatre arts, and most such programs offer courses or activities that bring exposure to interpretation, costumes, makeup, history, directing, and related studies.

Certainly, it is very important to study and practice one's craft. All successful performers in this area have worked long and hard to perfect their skills.

Students who want to be jugglers or other variety performers can start developing their skills in middle or high school. They might appear in school plays and shows and perform at parties, for church and community audiences, and in talent contests.

Where Jugglers Work

You may find jugglers or other variety performers working in a range of settings. The main centers for the highest-paid workers are Las Vegas, New York, and Hollywood. In large cities, they perform in stadiums, arenas, and other entertainment centers. In small towns and rural regions, performances may take place in schools, churches, or community centers. Performers may work in private homes, on street corners, or in shopping malls. They may also work in nightclubs, casinos, hotels, resorts, and restaurants. They perform for business meetings, conventions, promotions, and industrial and trade shows. They work at a wide range of social events and private parties.

Schools and colleges also offer some possibilities. Performers appear for fraternities and sororities, alumni organizations, special-interest groups, class reunions, and student bodies. College theatre groups also employ variety performers.

Organizations of all kinds book performers for meetings, fundraisers, children's parties, seasonal and holiday shows, parades, and other social and business events. Performers may find work at festivals, pageants, and fairs. They may travel with a carnival or circus or work on a cruise ship.

Variety performers may tour other countries as part of a company or with a USO group. They may appear in stage shows, at dinner theatres, in motion pictures, and in television shows and commercials. City parks, recreation departments, and amusement parks may hire jugglers for special events.

Getting Started in Juggling

The road to juggling typically begins on a small scale. Many performers start out in local charity or school programs. They may appear on talent shows. As they become better known, they audition for booking agents, producers, and other possible employers.

Trade journals, websites, and the yellow pages list jobs, theatrical agencies, and booking agents. Performers may get leads through a union or from friends and associates. They can make phone calls, send e-mail messages, write letters, and send resumes to potential employers. They must have a portfolio, and possibly videotapes or other media, to show prospective employers their record of performances.

Beginning variety performers in New York and other major cities may develop their acts in clubs, cabarets, and places that offer an open mike. Some entertainers perform on the street or at festivals.

Performers of this type have no guarantee of promotions or higher pay. Those with talent, determination, and luck may find openings for paid performances. Performers who become known locally may hire an agent to get bookings. A few may become celebrities. Others may be satisfied with steady work. Successful performers may work as solo acts, or they may start their own companies and advance to directing and producing. They may work as promoters or agents for other performers. Or they may work as performers on a part-time basis, sandwiching such activities around the requirements of a regular job.

International Jugglers' Association

A great source of information about this field, and an important provider of helpful services and support for practitioners, is the International Jugglers' Association (IJA). In operation since 1947, this nonprofit organization focuses on the advancement and promotion of juggling throughout the world. The IJA members represent a diverse array of skills, ages, and interests and span the range from amateurs to dedicated professionals. Membership is open to all who seek to share their love of juggling.

The mission of the IJA is to educate and render assistance to fellow jugglers. The organization provides accessible information pertaining to juggling and jugglers and records and maintains the history of juggling. It offers a wide variety of services, including an annual festival, workshops on topics of interest to members, and a magazine. Its online store offers videos, DVDs, and other merchandise.

The organization also produces videotapes of its events and instructional materials that members may purchase. *Juggler's World* magazine, which is published by the IJA, presents reviews of new videos, books, and props; descriptions of some of history's great juggling acts; interviews with the juggling world's most fascinating personalities; historical information; and more. Contact this organization as follows:

International Jugglers' Association
PO Box 112550
Carrollton, TX 70511
www.juggle.org

Another source of information about juggling is the Internet Juggling Database. This online site offers answers to frequently asked questions, basic details on learning to juggle, information on juggling clubs, schedules of forthcoming performances or events, a video database, articles on juggling, and more. Check it out at www.jugglingdb.com.

Financial Prospects

The earnings of jugglers vary with their skill, fame, employer, geographic region, and the kind and amount of work. They may receive anywhere from $25 to five-figure fees for one performance. Some of these entertainers earn more for an hour than others do for a week, but the pay for that one hour could be their entire income for a month. For union members, minimum pay rates are governed by agreements established by groups such as the American Guild of Variety Artists, the Screen Actors Guild, and the American Federation of Television and Radio Artists.

The American Guild of Variety Artists represents performers in nightclubs, circuses, and other places that present live entertainment. The American Federation of Television and Radio

Artists serves performers of live or taped radio and television programs.

The Screen Actors Guild serves performers in film, television, and commercials. The Associated Actors and Artists of America is an umbrella organization for the nine AFL-CIO unions that represent performing artists. All these unions negotiate contracts on wages, hours, and working conditions. Performers may sign individual contracts with special terms.

Union contracts also set terms for overtime and residuals (payment for reruns of films, commercials, and television shows in which the performers appear). The performers may also get a percentage of any sales from videos, DVDs, or other items such as dolls and games modeled after performers.

Because most performers are self-employed, they do not receive the fringe benefits other workers get. Although they work nights, weekends, and holidays, they seldom get extra pay. Union contracts may include pension plans, health insurance, and other aid. Entertainers who work for one employer long enough can collect unemployment insurance when the job ends. Sick leave and paid vacations are rare. National and local arts organizations sometimes offer group insurance and other benefits for those not covered by union contracts.

Most performers have other jobs. Many take whatever kind of work they can get to fill in between jobs. They may sell their tapes, films, DVDs, books, or other products.

Future Prospects

While jobs in this field can be exciting, the prospects for employment are limited. There is no accurate estimate of the number of performers or the number of jobs available. The unemployment rate is very high—perhaps 60 to 65 percent for these workers. The competition is stiff. The number of job seekers is always greater than the number of jobs.

Most entertainers work only part-time. At best they make only a modest living. Only a very few become rich and famous.

Words from the Pros

Introducing Jack Kalvan

Jack Kalvan is an entertainer who is based in California but who works all over the world. His training includes a number of comedy, acting, and dance classes, including Greg Dean's Stand-Up Comedy Workshop in Los Angeles.

Jack has been interested in entertaining since childhood. At the age of twelve, he unwittingly determined his fate by teaching himself to juggle three balls. Juggling quickly became his main love and obsession. Jack honed his juggling skills for many years while fulfilling his more scholarly ambitions. He earned a degree in mechanical engineering from Carnegie Mellon University in Pittsburgh and then took a job in robotics at IBM Research in Yorktown Heights, New York, where he actually worked on building and teaching a robot to juggle. He eventually quit that job to pursue his true love, a career in juggling. Since starting his career, Jack has performed thousands of shows in hundreds of cities around the world. He has appeared on television shows such as the "Drew Carey Show" and "Days of Our Lives."

"I had so much fun practicing juggling, I spent most of my free time doing it," he says. "I was becoming pretty well known by other jugglers. When people offered me money to juggle, I could not turn it down. While I was working at IBM in New York, many of my friends were doing street shows. It looked like fun, and they were making pretty good money at it. I did some of my first shows passing the hat in New York's Central Park and Washington Square."

Now, much of his time is spent at home. But when he does work, he makes enough money to live on the rest of the time. About twice a month he spends a day on the phone calling up agents and trying to get work. There are times when he works every day for long periods. At one time, when he was performing extensively at colleges, his days were mostly spent driving to the next show and sleeping in hotels. Now he is usually employed for one show at a time.

He has enjoyed performing in Atlantic City and also in Japan. He has worked frequently on numerous cruise ships. When not performing, he periodically develops new shows. This involves a substantial amount of time writing new routines and rehearsing them, as well as writing and designing new promotional materials.

"The best thing about this career is that I get paid to juggle," he says. "And I am paid well enough that I can spend most of my time at home with my family, doing whatever I want. I seldom have to get up early, and I don't have to work in an office. I am self-employed and can take the shows I want and not take the shows I don't want."

He says that at first the travel was very exciting, but now it's one of the things he likes least because he usually doesn't have time to go sightseeing.

Jack worked with a partner, Rick Rubenstein, for about ten years doing a two-man show called *Clockwork*. The two met in college and became friends and then partners. Later, Jack made the transition to performing exclusively solo shows.

"I would advise that you not expect to become famous or wealthy," he says. "Remember that it may take years before you have a good show. Be original; the world doesn't need any more corny juggling acts. Research, but do not copy what others have done. Do what you are good at. Never be satisfied with your show; always strive for improvement."

Introducing the Raspyni Brothers

Dan Holzman and Barry Friedman present themselves as the Raspyni Brothers. While they are not actually brothers, they are a successful juggling duo. The two partners met in a park in the 1980s when they were twenty years old, and they quickly formed a partnership to perform comedy/juggling shows. After more than two decades of entertaining, their credits include "The Tonight Show," a command performance for the president, "Circus of the Stars," and the "Jerry Lewis MDA Telethon." They have performed as the opening act for Tom Jones, Robin Williams, Billy Crystal, and other famous entertainers and have also won several juggling championships.

For their previous jobs, Dan sat in a room and sorted x-rays. Barry drove a forklift in a small warehouse. "These jobs had a tremendous bearing on our career paths because we knew that if we didn't find something more interesting and challenging to do with our lives, they would just bring us more x-rays and pallets," Dan says.

Today, they spend much of their time on airplanes flying around the country as well as to other nations. On show days, they meet with clients and make sure that they understand exactly what is expected of them as performers.

When at home, they meet and talk about new markets, new routines, and new projects to make themselves more popular. They also practice juggling, usually for an hour each day.

Asked what they like most, the two list the travel, the money, the excitement of performing, meeting and working with famous celebrities (because it humanizes them and makes their level seem attainable), being on television, seeing new places, staying in world-class resorts, getting standing ovations, seeing people laugh so hard that they have tears in their eyes, doing encores, sending postcards from the Caribbean to all the people who said they would never make anything of themselves, and eating in New Orleans.

The main shortcoming is the need to be away from home so much. "Our life is the textbook case of 'the greener grass' theory," Barry says. "We usually find ourselves either at home or on the road and wishing for the other. Too often, friends get married on weekends when we are traveling. Too bad more people don't get married on Tuesday nights; we're usually available!"

The two advise others to work hard and be creative. They offer these tips: "Don't ever take no for an answer; someone will say yes if you keep asking. Believe in yourself. Don't ever treat life like a rehearsal. Do what you love, and if you are good at it, the money will follow. The beaten path has already been taken, so blaze a new one for yourself. Don't ever be content with what you have done; there is only one time to quit, and God lets you know when that time has come."

Introducing Jonathon Wee

Jonathon Wee is a San Francisco–based entertainer. He has a bachelor of arts degree in economics from Luther College, a small, private liberal arts college in Iowa.

Jonathon is largely self-taught. He learned primarily from going to juggling festivals, seeing other jugglers, and juggling with them. He started out by learning to juggle three bean bags when he was in eighth grade at the age of thirteen. A woman was teaching a few people to juggle, and he thought it looked like fun, so he joined in and was immediately hooked. He spent much of his spare time just standing in a corner of the room, or wherever he could find space, juggling for hours. Then he taught two friends, and the three of them started doing small shows for birthday parties and picnics. Their first real job of any distinction was at the Minnesota Renaissance Festival when he was fifteen.

"I was first fascinated with the juggling itself," he says. "The feeling of satisfaction, of learning something that seemed impossible but soon became easier and easier, was compelling. And there were no boundaries—just so many possibilities. Hundreds of tricks with three balls, then working on four balls, then tricks with four, then five, and so on. And then when that got boring, all I had to do was pick up rings or clubs (the things that look like bowling pins) or flaming torches, and it was all new again."

He also found juggling was a fun thing to do with others. "You could teach each other, show off what you had learned, or challenge the other person or people to do what you can do. The next step was cooperating and learning to pass between two or three or more people. That group effort and accomplishment was a fun way to meet and bond with people. But I became truly attracted to it as a profession when I got onstage and realized that I could make people laugh and applaud. And the fact that I could actually get paid for it was almost too good to be true!"

One summer during college, Jonathon had a job laying sod. He remembers it as the most miserable working experience he had ever had. It was dirty, back-breaking work, but the experience helped him realize that by comparison, juggling was something really wonderful. He still had some thoughts about a more main-stream job after college, but he knew that his college education was at least going to keep him out of doing hard labor, and he was glad about that.

Once he made the commitment, Jonathon was able to build a successful career. He and his partner often work for corporate clients, juggling their products while making jokes or references to the industry or company. They also perform at comedy clubs, on cruise ships, at NBA halftime shows, and other venues. Most of their performances take place evenings and weekends.

"I love making people laugh," he says. "I love being able to travel and meet interesting people in exotic and fun places. And I love the possibilities. I never know what the next phone call is going to be—it could be a great new gig, a trip around the world, a spot on a television show, or an audition for our own television show or movie—anything!"

Introducing Doubble Troubble Jugglers

Nick and Alex Karvounis are based in Las Vegas but work all over the world, including shows on cruise ships.

Both earned bachelor of arts degrees in film and television production from New York University. The two began juggling in elementary school when their gym teacher taught the entire fourth grade juggling during class. Of the hundreds of children he taught over the years, Alex and Nick were the only ones to continue juggling as more than just as a hobby. On weekends during middle and high school, they practiced juggling with many amateurs and professionals at the Baltimore Jugglers Club. By this time, the two were already performing a twenty-minute magic and juggling show for children's birthday parties. They found they enjoyed making people laugh.

"I think, in the long run, the reason we continue to perform our comedy and variety show is the satisfaction and joy you get when you step out onto stage and make a theatre full of thousands of people laugh," Nick says. "I remember seeing an article on Anthony Gatto, another juggler from Baltimore, and his job in Las Vegas. I remember seeing a photo of him on stage juggling seven rings. I said 'Wow!' And that's another reason I love to perform. I love to see people walk away from our show and say 'Wow . . . amazing.' Pure satisfaction!"

After performing at children's birthday parties, conventions, and other events in the Baltimore area on the weekends during high school, Nick and Alex went to college. Their four years at New York University in the heart of the Big Apple proved rewarding. During the summers they worked at a resort in the Poconos, where they served as camp counselors during the day and entertained at night. The first time they performed onstage was as an opening act for a comedian. The manager asked them to do fifteen minutes, but they lost track of time and ran over thirty minutes. Nevertheless, the pair was still invited back.

They also began to experiment with street performing. "Street performing is where an act can really become refined," Nick says. "It is when you are out on the street that you really learn how to keep an audience. If your show isn't interesting enough or funny enough or exciting enough, the audience will leave. I am truly convinced that the street is what makes or breaks an act. The street will separate the good from the bad, the strong from the weak. The street is where we learned to deal with hecklers in the crowd. This experience with street performing and passing the hat for a few bucks is where we really learned to appreciate the audience. The only reason we as entertainers survive is because the audience decides that we should survive. The second the audience stops liking you, you're dead."

From New York and the Poconos, they moved on to theme parks, such as Bush Gardens in Williamsburg and Walt Disney World in Orlando, Florida. After relocating to Orlando for work with Disney, they were offered their first job on a cruise ship.

"Cruise ships are definitely the place to be," Nick says. "The theatres that we perform in are more beautiful than most showrooms in Las Vegas. They are state-of-the-art theatres that hold more than a thousand people and have forty-foot stage ceilings, orchestra pits, and millions of dollars worth of lights and sets. On a seven-day cruise with RCCL [Royal Carribean Cruise Line], you can expect to see two celebrity entertainers, two large-scale-production shows, and three to four other variety artists. Every act is professional and entertaining. Our work on the cruise ships is very rewarding and exciting."

Nick and Alex find that many people think their jobs are easy, but it's not just a matter of putting on a one-hour show and then sitting back for the rest of week. Even though a show may last a fraction of a normal workday, there is much more that goes on behind the scenes.

When they are between contracts, much of the day is spent making phone calls and sending out promotional materials. Many phone calls are made to their agents and prospective clients, searching for that next booking. They also stay busy on the computer, designing new brochures and updating materials for their portfolio, sometimes taking days or weeks to achieve the exact look they want for the client. With the use of desktop-publishing software, Alex and Nick have mastered the design of new promotional materials directed specifically to a prospective client, adding that personal touch to each piece. For instance, when they were designing promotional materials to submit to the National Basketball Association, they added NBA photos along with pictures of their act to make the materials more personalized.

Any given day may continue with the unexpected as well. An agent may call and ask if they can send promotional material to a client for a last-minute job. Everything in their office stops so that they can send out a package overnight halfway around the world. One hour later, after a long line at the post office, they are back in the office with other projects still waiting for them. When evening comes, they may still be working.

"People wonder why we don't stop at five o'clock. It may be quitting time in Las Vegas, but halfway around the world in Tokyo, there is an agent who needs to talk to us. We have come to find that there are no office hours in this business as well as no weekends or holidays. When the phone rings, the phone rings, and if you don't pick it up you may miss an important job. And it has happened to us before, so we quickly learned our lesson."

Another part of their work is trying out new routines at the gym or on the racquetball court. It may takes months to perfect a new routine with new props and choreography. A typical rehearsal might run an hour. Through trial and error, they begin to find what feels right and looks right. They note that the process can be frustrating because when they are learning new tricks, their timing may be off, and they may drop things. But all the hard work pays off when the trick is perfected and applause and laughter come from the audience.

Their act includes a good deal of comedy. Some of their humorous material comes by accident. If they are in the middle of a show and someone slips or says the wrong word, they may turn it into comedy.

They say the most rewarding part of the job is the actual show. "It is exciting to see and hear an audience laugh and respond to the juggling and comedy," Nick says. "The travel also makes for a unique and interesting part of the job. We are in a position to do what we love to do and see parts of the world that we thought we'd only see in history books or on the Travel Channel.

Our performing has taken us to nearly every continent on the earth and seeing and meeting people of every culture and background. It has been a learning experience far beyond anything we could have expected, which is what makes us enjoy taking our show on the road."

They add that while traveling may bring excitement, it can also become tiresome. Waiting in crowded airports and carrying luggage are definite downsides.

"There is more to performing than just knowing how to juggle," Nick says. "There have been some great jugglers in the past who couldn't entertain an audience. The novelty of juggling wears off quickly, so you must come up with something unique to keep the audience's interest. To keep your show interesting, you must make the audience like and relate to you onstage. Finally, the most important thing is that you have to enjoy what you are doing. If not, move on and try something else. Good luck!"

Other Variety Performers

Along with jugglers, a number of other career areas involve some type of variety performance. In addition to those of actors and musical performers (covered later in this book), they include the following:

- Acrobat
- Amusement-park entertainer
- Announcer
- Aquatic performer
- Dancer
- Disc jockey
- Impersonator
- Magician's assistant
- Mime
- Narrator
- Psychic

- Puppeteer
- Ring conductor
- Rodeo performer
- Show girl
- Stuntman or stuntwoman
- Talk-show host
- Thrill performer
- Ventriloquist
- Wire walker

Making It as a Mime

A mime is a performer who practices pantomime, which is the art of conveying stories by bodily movements alone; no words are spoken. Sometimes this art is called *mime* for short, as is a person who practices it.

Mime performances can be seen frequently as practiced by members of amateur theatre companies, but relatively few men and women make a career of it. Like jugglers or other variety artists, many mimes pursue this art as a hobby or part-time career.

Those who love mime feel it offers a special challenge, since performers may use only their skill with bodily movement or facial expressions to convey emotions or other concepts.

Marcel Marceau

Without doubt, the world's most acclaimed mime is Marcel Marceau. Born in Strasbourg, France, Marceau became interested in mime as a child and eventually made it his career. He studied under another famous mime, Etienne Decroux, and ended up becoming famous not only in Europe, but also in North America and elsewhere.

Marceau created Bip, a character in a striped pullover and battered opera hat who became his alter ego. Bip's encounters with people, animals, and objects became the stuff of legend in the entertainment world.

Marceau has been performing in the United States and Canada since the 1950s, both in live performances and on television. His awards are too numerous to list. The French government awarded him its highest honor, the Legion of Honor, and he holds honorary doctorates from Ohio State University, Linfield College, Princeton University, and the University of Michigan.

If you are interested in exploring a career as a mime, you certainly will want to watch him perform and study his style. Even if not, anyone can enjoy his wonderful performances. For additional information, including details about upcoming performances, visit the website offered by the Marcel Marceau Foundation at www.marceau.org.

Learning Mime

To learn the art of mime, consider taking classes. Sometimes you can find workshops or classes offered by a local college, university, or individual performer. A few organizations specialize in such activities.

The American Mime Theatre, located in New York, teaches a unique approach based on an identified balance of playwriting, acting, moving, pantomime, and theatrical equipment. This approach differs from that of the French schools and is taught only at the American Mime Theatre. For information, contact:

The American Mime Theatre
61 Fourth Avenue
New York, NY 10003
www.americanmime.org

Mime Theatre Studio, located in North Hollywood, California, offers weekly classes in mime theatre throughout the year. Beginners complete an introductory level made up of six classes. After that, they may attend classes at more advanced levels for as long as desired. Short-term workshops are also offered.

Students at this school learn the fundamentals of the art, basic physical and dramatic skills, specialized movement skills, "physicalization" of emotion, and stylization techniques. In the course of their studies, they are exposed to techniques developed by Marcel Marceau, Etienne Decroux, Polish master Stefan Niedzialkowski, and others. For more information, visit the Mime Theatre Studio website at www.mimetheatrestudio.com.

Venturing into Ventriloquism

Another specialty in the area of variety performance is ventriloquism. Performers who develop this skill project their voices so that the sound seems to be coming from somewhere else, typically from a dummy that forms the other half of a comedy act.

While some performers specialize as ventriloquists, others combine this approach with other types of comedy. Some use it as a gimmick to deliver religious messages or other material.

If you'd like to explore this area, consider getting in touch with someone who is a practicing ventriloquist and asking for tips. Or take a class or workshop. A good place to get started is the International Ventriloquists' Association. This group offers an annual festival and publishes a magazine, *Distant Voices*. It also provides helpful networking opportunities.

For more information, contact:

International Ventriloquists' Association
PO Box 17153
Las Vegas, NV 89114
www.inquista.com

Here is your next birth-name challenge: Jennifer Anastassakis.

For More Information

Daily Variety Magazine
360 Park Avenue South
New York, NY 10010
or
5700 Wilshire Boulevard, Suite 120
Los Angeles, CA 90036
www.variety.com
   Daily tabloid for the entertainment industry

International Jugglers' Association (IJA)
PO Box 112550
Carrollton, TX 70511
www.juggle.org

Internet Juggling Database (IJDb)
www.jugglingdb.com

Screen Actors Guild (SAG)
360 Madison Avenue, Twelfth Floor
New York, NY 10017
or
5757 Wilshire Boulevard
Hollywood, CA 90036
www.sag.com

CHAPTER SIX

Actors

I n our society, actors are special people. Those who have reached the top of the profession are constantly in the limelight. You can't turn on the television or look at a magazine without seeing their faces and learning (perhaps more than you want) about their lives.

Gracing Stage and Screen

Regardless of their level of success, actors share a common task: playing roles or parts in comedic, musical, or dramatic productions. This includes performances on the stage, on television, in motion pictures, and on radio. In an attempt to both communicate and entertain, actors utilize speech, gestures, movement, and body language. In this way they operate as the principals who tell us a story.

The work of actors begins long before they perform in front of an audience or camera. Before the actual production, they analyze the theme of the play or story, study the script, scrutinize the character they are to play, memorize the lines, gain a concrete understanding of the director's viewpoint, become familiar with the cues that bring them on and off the stage, and often spend long, tedious hours in rehearsals.

In some ways, the mediums in which actors work (whether on the stage, in movies, or on television) determines to what extent they must prepare for their parts. For example, performers assigned roles in musical comedies played onstage may not only have to memorize speaking lines, but also to sing, dance, and carry out other functions in connection with their parts, which may mean taking vocal or dancing instructions in order to fulfill the requirements of the role. Their roles may require them to speak with appropriate accents or speech patterns associated with the characters or the locale of the production, or to learn distinctive physical movements and gestures that are specific to the characters they are playing. In some cases, they may be required to apply appropriate makeup, although in most cases, makeup artists are employed to accomplish this.

Usually, actors who perform in stage shows rehearse for longer periods of time than do radio or television performers. Lines, actions, and cues must be perfect before the public sees the show. Musicals and stage plays may run for weeks or even years, although the people assuming the various roles may change. Rehearsals for a drama production may run about four weeks, while musicals may take one or two additional weeks.

Radio performers are not required to practice as extensively as stage or film performers must since they can read their lines without having to memorize them. However, some rehearsal is usually required because they must be sure to put a lot of emotion into their voices so that listeners may gain an understanding and appreciation for the characters without ever seeing them.

Weekly television shows and commercials are frequently filmed or taped in short periods of time. Many of the television programs currently scheduled are weekly series with all rehearsals and filming accomplished in six days or less. Special shows or films made exclusively for television take much more preparation than weekly shows. Since most television productions are prerecorded on film or videotape, the rehearsal and filming techniques are similar to those used in the movie industry.

Generally, movie actors don't rehearse a movie from the beginning to the end. They work on small segments, one at a time, and the cameras roll to film these short scenes. Later, the film editors put the scenes in proper order.

Relatively few actors achieve star status in any of the mediums of stage, motion pictures, or television. A somewhat larger number are well-known, experienced performers who are frequently cast in supporting roles. Many successful actors continue to accept these small roles, including commercials and product endorsements. Actors who accept nonspeaking parts are usually called *day players* or *extras*. Sometimes hundreds of extras are hired for movies—especially for scenes in which there are many people assembled for a large-scale event (such as a battle or a crowd scene).

To become a movie extra, one must usually be listed with a casting agency, such as Central Casting, a no-fee agency that supplies extras to all the major movie studios in Hollywood. Applicants are accepted only when the number of persons of a particular type on the list—for example, athletic young women, old men, or small children—is below the foreseeable need.

Between engagements, actors refine and develop their talents by taking vocal, dancing, and acting lessons. They also may make personal appearances, accept offers to perform benefit shows, or teach drama courses to aspiring actors.

Demand for Actors

Performers are hired for stage shows, appearances in film, commercials, and parts on radio and television. New York and Hollywood are the most likely places to land acting jobs. Next most likely would be cities such as Boston, Chicago, Seattle, Dallas, Miami, Vancouver, Minneapolis, and San Francisco.

However, most large cities have several theatre groups. Even smaller towns usually have acting groups that offer a chance to gain some experience and employment. These include little theatres, children's theatres, and regional and community theatres. Summer-stock tours take actors all around the United States and Canada.

An Actor's Life

Although ordinary people tend to focus on the glamour involved, the life of an actor is usually an uncertain one. Professional actors always face the anxiety of unsteady employment and the disappointment of rejections. And because there are often long periods of unemployment between jobs, acting demands patience and total commitment.

Performers must be available for constant rehearsals that may be stressful and physically and mentally exhausting—a situation that can be exacerbated by script or cast changes. Performers often spend several weeks rehearsing their parts, and some rehearsals may be scheduled on weekends, holidays, and evenings. Those having small roles may wait for hours before being called to rehearse their parts.

Rehearsals may take place amid the clutter of electricians, camera operators, painters, carpenters, and stagehands. Heavy costumes and hot lights may add to the stress. Deadlines loom in this business, too, and performers may be called upon to accomplish quite a bit in a very short period of time. In fact, a performer may rehearse one production in the morning and afternoon and perform another every evening.

The type of role being played often determines the amount of physical exertion required. For some roles, performers move about a great deal when walking or running, riding horses, dancing, or performing hazardous stunts, although a professionally trained stunt person usually undertakes the more dangerous stunts.

Considerable traveling is often required of performers employed by theatrical road companies. These individuals perform the same play in a series of locations. They frequently give an evening performance in one city and spend the following day traveling to the theatre where the next performance is to be given. They must adjust to the varying facilities and equipment available in each theatre. Movie personnel are also required to travel to sites that have been chosen as film locations.

The physical surroundings of actors performing in stage productions can range from modern, air-conditioned, comfortable, and well-equipped theatres to those that are old and have inadequate facilities. Backstage areas of many theatres are crowded, dusty, drafty, and poorly ventilated. Actors may be provided private dressing rooms or apply their makeup and change costumes in areas shared by several other performers.

The Path to an Acting Career

What path leads to an acting career? Aspiring actors should take part in high school and college plays and work with community theatres, summer stock, regional theatre, dinner theatre, children's theatre, and other acting groups for experience. In fact, any stage work is useful. Formal dramatic training or acting experience is generally necessary and is definitely advantageous, although some people do enter the field without it. Most people take college courses in theatre, arts, drama, and dramatic literature. Many experienced actors get additional formal training to learn new skills and improve old ones. Training can be obtained at dramatic arts schools in New York and Los Angeles, among other locations, and at colleges and universities.

Academic programs in drama and theatre are offered at both undergraduate and graduate levels through several approaches. College drama curricula usually include courses in the liberal arts, stage speech and movement, directing, playwriting, play production, design, and history of drama, as well as practical courses in acting. Other important areas include literature, dramatic arts, music, dance, communications, and English.

At the University of Kentucky, students interested in acting have degree options that include a bachelor of arts degree (B.A.), a bachelor of fine arts degree (B.F.A.) with a concentration in acting, a bachelor of fine arts degree with a concentration in design and technology, and a master of arts degree (M.A.).

The B.F.A. program is open only to students who have demonstrated special abilities in acting, and auditions are required for admission. This program offers a traditional liberal arts approach to the study of acting. In addition to general degree requirements, students complete courses such as the following:

- History of the Theatre I and II
- Acting I: Fundamentals of Acting
- Fundamentals of Design and Production
- Vocal Production for the Stage I and II
- Script Analysis
- Acting II: Scene Study (Realism)
- Acting III: Scene Study (Styles)
- Audition Techniques
- Theatre Movement I and II
- Topics in Movement
- Acting IV: Classical Styles
- Acting V: European Realism
- Dialects
- Production Practicum

Students also complete a senior project as well as participating in one or more summer productions in professional theatre.

For more information about this program, contact:

University of Kentucky
Department of Theatre
114 Fine Arts Building
Lexington, KY 40506
www.uky.edu/FineArts/Theatre

Canada's York University offers several degree programs related to drama, including a bachelor of fine arts honours program where students concentrate on studio work in performance or production.

To earn a B.F.A. honours degree, students complete 120 credits, including 36 theatre credits at any level; 24 theatre credits at the upper-division level, with at least half in studio; 12 fine arts electives that are not in theatre; 6 non–fine arts elective credits; 18 general education credits or approved substitutes; and 24 credits in elective courses.

Here are some sample course descriptions for this program:

- **Acting** (introductory course). An introduction to what a student may experience as a performer, it concentrates on verbal and nonverbal communication both in an ensemble situation and as a soloist. Reading and written work are an essential part of the course.
- **Acting** (second course). A continuing exploration of the techniques and exercises commenced in the introductory course. Particular emphasis on script analysis and scene study, with a concentration on monologues and two-handed scenes, as well as a continued emphasis on journal writing. (optional)
- **Production** (introductory course). Through exposure to a variety of technical areas, students will develop production-crew work habits and build a basic vocabulary in production and design. Participation on crews is a requirement of this course.
- **Production** (second course). A continuation of the exposure begun in the introductory course but in considerably more depth and detail. Required for those interested in production and an option for all theatre majors.
- **Theatre Survey.** A foundational encounter with diverse forms of theatre from different epochs, integrating analytical reading with studio explorations of performance possibilities through scene study and rehearsed stagings and consideration of aspects of production and design.

For information about overall program requirements, contact:

York University
4700 Keele Street
Toronto ON M3J 1P3
Canada
www.yorku.ca/finearts

Another college drama and acting program is New Jersey's Centenary College, which offers a B.A. in theatre arts. Students who enroll in this program have the opportunity to develop skills in a working professional theatre while pursuing a broad-based liberal arts education. In addition to basic liberal arts courses, theatre students take classes in acting, dance, voice, and stagecraft.

Of special note is the opportunity to participate in the Centenary Stage Company, where students work in professional productions as actors, crew, stage management, and front-house personnel. Working alongside veterans of stage and screen, students gain exposure to the practical side of professional theatre. Those who are interested in joining the actors' union may also earn credit toward obtaining union cards.

Second- and third-year students may elect to study acting in several affiliate studios in New York City, and the college's proximity to New York allows for a staff of instructors, artists, and designers drawn from the ranks of working professionals.

For more information, contact:

Centenary College
400 Jefferson Street
Hackettstown, NJ 07840
www.centenarystageco.org

For those with a bachelor's degree, a challenging possibility is provided by the Actors Studio Drama School. This three-year intensive program is dedicated to training professional artists in the fields of playwriting, directing, and acting. Students who successfully complete the program are awarded a master of fine arts degree in theatre.

The program is rooted in "The Method," an approach developed by Constantin Stanislavski in Russia and later adapted in the United States through the Group Theatre and the Actors Studio. A major goal of the program is to produce "theatre artists who have access to emotional truth and moment-to-moment reality while maintaining a sense of stagecraft and professionalism." The Actors Studio Drama School is a joint program of New School University and the Actors Studio.

More details are available at:

Actors Studio Drama School
151 Bank Street
New York, NY 10014
www.newschool.edu

Getting Started

Once you have your degree and some basic experience, the best way to get started is to make use of opportunities close to you, then build upon them. For example, regional theatre experience may help in obtaining work in a large city such as New York or Los Angeles. Modeling experience may also be helpful.

In addition to a sincere interest in and love of acting, actors must have talent, training, poise, stage presence, the ability to move an audience, the ability to follow directions, an appealing physical appearance, and experience in order to succeed. Other important elements for success include hard work, dedication, self-confidence, versatility, ambition, good health, patience, commitment, stamina, the ability to memorize, the ability to withstand adverse conditions, perseverance, drive, determination, desire, discipline, and the ability to handle emotional tension and disappointment. Those who are self-conscious or withdrawn will not make it.

The length of a performer's working life depends largely on training, skills, versatility, and perseverance. Some actors continue working throughout their lives. Many, however, leave the occupation after a short time because they cannot find enough work to make a living.

Compensation for Actors

While superstars make tremendous amounts of money, the incomes of most actors are modest. Median annual earnings of salaried actors were $23,470 in 2002, according to the U.S. Department of Labor. The middle 50 percent earned between $15,320 and $53,320. The lowest 10 percent earned less than $13,330, and the highest 10 percent earned more than $106,360. Minimum salaries, hours of work, and other conditions of employment are covered in collective bargaining agreements between the producers and the unions representing workers. The Actors' Equity Association (Equity) represents stage actors; the Screen Actors Guild (SAG) covers actors in motion pictures, including television, commercials, and films; and the American Federation of Television and Radio Artists (AFTRA) represents performers who work in television and radio studios. While these unions generally determine minimum salaries, any actor or director may negotiate for a salary higher than the minimum.

Under terms of a joint SAG and AFTRA contract covering all unionized workers, motion picture and television actors with speaking parts earned a minimum daily rate of $678 or $2,352 for a five-day week as of July 2003. Actors also receive contributions to health and pension plans and additional compensation for reruns and foreign telecasts of productions in which they appear.

According to Equity, the minimum weekly salary for actors in Broadway productions as of June 2003 was $1,354. Actors in off-Broadway theatres received minimums ranging from $479 to $557 a week as of October 2003, depending on the seating capacity of the theatre. Regional theatres that operate under an Equity agreement pay actors $531 to $800 per week. For touring productions, actors receive an additional $111 per day for living expenses ($117 per day in larger, higher-cost cities).

Some well-known actors earn well above the minimum. Their salaries may be many times the figures cited, creating the false impression that all actors are highly paid. For example, of the nearly one hundred thousand SAG members, only about fifty might be considered stars. The average income that SAG members earn from acting—less than $5,000 a year—is low because employment is erratic. Therefore, most actors must supplement their incomes by holding jobs in other occupations.

Many actors who work more than a set number of weeks per year are covered by a union health, welfare, and pension fund, which provides hospitalization insurance. Employers who hire Equity actors contribute to this fund. Under some employment conditions, Equity and AFTRA members receive paid vacations and sick leave.

How About the Future?

Employment of actors, producers, and directors is expected to grow about as fast as the average for all occupations through 2012. As in the past, large numbers of people will aspire to enter these professions. At the same time, many will leave the field early. Their experience will show them that the work—when it is available—is hard, the hours are long, and the pay is low. Competition for jobs will be stiff, in part because the large number of highly trained and talented actors auditioning for roles generally exceeds the number of parts that become available. Only performers with the most stamina and talent will find regular employment.

On the positive side, expanding cable and satellite television operations, increasing production and distribution of major studio and independent films, and continued growth and development of interactive media, such as direct-for-Web movies and videos, should increase demand for actors and related workers.

However, greater emphasis on national, rather than local, entertainment productions may restrict employment opportunities in the broadcasting industry.

Venues for live entertainment—such as Broadway and off-Broadway theatres, touring productions, repertory theatres in many major metropolitan areas, theme parks, and resorts—are expected to offer many job opportunities. Prospects in these venues are more variable, though, because they tend to fluctuate with economic conditions.

Finding Acting Jobs

How do you land acting jobs? Armed with your college degree, basic knowledge of the acting business, and some experience, you'll need to prepare a portfolio that highlights your qualifications, acting history, and special skills. This will take the form of a resume and "head shots," or photographic portraits. You will need to have photos taken by a professional photographer, one who shows you to your best advantage. These are the essential tools of your trade. Attach your resume to the back of your picture with one staple at the upper left- and right-hand corners.

Once you have your portfolio ready, you can start making the rounds at casting offices, ad agencies, and producers' and agents' offices. Several trade newspapers contain casting information, ads for part-time jobs, information about shows, and other pertinent data about what's going on in the industry. Publications of interest include:

Daily Variety Magazine (www.variety.com)
The Hollywood Reporter (www.hollywoodreporter.com)
TDR/The Drama Review (http://mitpress.mit.edu)
Journal of American Drama and Theatre
    (http://web.gc.cuny.edu/mestc/jadt.htm)
Theater (www.yale.edu/drama/publications/theater)

Once you drop off your resumes and head shots, don't just sit at home waiting for that phone call or e-mail message. It's wise to stay in contact—stop by and say hello. Check in by phone every week to see if any opportunities are available for you. If you are currently in a show, send prospective employers a flyer. It shows them that you are a working actor.

When you get past this initial stage and actually win an audition, there are some things you should remember.

Audition Tips

Here are some words of advice for aspiring actors.

- Be prepared.
- Be familiar with the piece—read it beforehand and choose the parts you'd like to try out for.
- Go for it—don't hold back.
- Speak loudly and clearly—project your voice to reach the back of the room.
- Take chances.
- Try not to be the one going first—if you can observe others, you can see what they do, correct their mistakes, and get a feel for the script.
- Be enthusiastic and confident.
- Keep auditioning—even if you don't get any parts, you are getting invaluable experience that is bound to pay off.

So, when do you get an agent? Not right away, anyway. You don't need an agent to find audition opportunities. There are many parts you can audition for that do not require an agent—theatre, nonunion films, union films. However, most commercials are cast through agencies, so you would most likely need an agent to land one of those. While waiting to be chosen for a part, acting hopefuls often take jobs that afford a flexible schedule and money to live on, such as waiting tables, bartending, or driving taxis.

Words from the Pros

Introducing Jennifer Aquino

Jennifer Aquino grew up in Cerritos, California. She got her first taste of acting at St. Linus elementary school in Norwalk, where she played the leading role of the princess in *Beyond the Horizon*. Continuing with success in this area, she received the Performing Arts Award while attending Whitney High School. Subsequently, she graduated from the University of California–Los Angeles, where she studied theatre and dance and received a bachelor of arts degree in economics. (After all, the entertainment industry is a business!) As a member of the dance team, she was a UCLA cheerleader for three years. In addition to cheering for UCLA's football and basketball teams, she also entered national dance-team competitions.

Following her college graduation, she got her first break playing Eolani, the wife of Dr. Jacoby in David Lynch's television series "Twin Peaks," a result of her very first audition. Then she got an agent and joined the Screen Actors Guild. She has performed in various theatrical productions since then and was a founding member of Theatre Geo. She is also active with the East West Players network of actors.

"I remember performing at family gatherings ever since I was a little kid," says Jennifer. "I always enjoyed being in the spotlight. To me, acting is like a child's game of pretend, something I always enjoyed. I see it as a career where I can earn a lot of money while having a lot of fun. At the same time I am entertaining people, impacting them, making them think, making them feel certain emotions, educating them, and helping them escape from their current lives."

Like most actors, she needed a day job to keep income coming in. For her it was a career in the health-care industry working for Kaiser Foundation Health Plan. She then became a health-care consultant for a major accounting firm, Deloitte & Touche. She was a good employee, and her managers were cooperative in letting her go out on auditions. After a few years, she realized that she was working too many hours, and she made the tough decision to quit her day job to focus entirely on acting.

Acting itself also requires long hours, but she is willing to make that commitment. The workload sometimes involves working seven days a week, including mornings, afternoons, evenings, and weekends. Along with the time spent on the creative side of acting is the need to focus on business concerns—talking to agents or managers, networking, attending seminars, meeting people, and sending photos to casting directors, producers, directors, or writers. She also tries to keep her stress level down and take care of herself by getting enough sleep, exercising, eating healthily, and having some relaxation time.

"What I like most about my work is that I am making a living doing what I absolutely love to do and that I am pursuing my passion in life," Jennifer says. "Not too many people in this world can say that." She adds that the least appealing aspect of her work is what might be called the political side. She feels that it's not always the best actor who gets the job, but sometimes it's more a matter of personal connections or other such factors.

Aquino advises anyone who is considering acting as a career to pursue their dreams and be persistent. "But do that only if it's something you absolutely love to do, and there's nothing else in the world you would rather do," she says. "Pursue the creative as well as the business side of acting. Don't let anyone stop you from doing what you want to do. And always keep up your craft by continuing your training."

Introducing Gonzo Schexnayder

Before getting into show business, Gonzo Schexnayder earned a bachelor's degree in journalism and advertising at Louisiana State University. He attended various acting classes at LSU and Monterey Peninsula College in Monterey, California. He also attended Chicago's Second City Training Center for over a year and the

Actors' Center following that. He is a member of both SAG and AFTRA.

"I had always wanted to do stand-up comedy but didn't pursue it until graduating from college, when I began working with an improvisational comedy group," he says. "Four months later, the military sent me to Monterey, California, for language training. While there, I did my first staged reading and my first show. I'd never felt such elation as when I performed. Nothing in my life had given me the sheer thrill and rush that I experienced by creating a character and maintaining that throughout a given period of time. Nothing else mattered but that moment on stage, my other actors, and the scene we were performing."

After completing the language training program, he returned to Louisiana. There he began the long process of introspection about his career choices and what he wanted to do. He began to audition locally and started reading and studying acting. He still had not made the jump to being an actor but was merely investigating the possibility.

One night, while watching an interview with actor John Goodman, Gonzo realized how important acting had become to him. He knew that it possibly meant a life of macaroni and cheese and Ramen noodles, but he realized that until that moment, nothing else had made him as happy or as motivated. While he believed he had the skills and the drive to make it in advertising or some other career, he decided that acting was his only logical choice.

"Whether it's rehearsing a show, performing improvisation in front of an audience, or even auditioning for a commercial, it's fun," he says. "If you can separate the sense of rejection most actors feel from not getting a part, auditioning for anything becomes your job. Rehearsing becomes your life. Just as a carpenter's job is building a house, as actor, I look at my job as building my performance. The final product is there for me to look at and admire (if executed well), but the path to that product is the thrill."

Gonzo says he loves the process of acting and sometimes just the fast-paced, eclectic nature of the business. There is always something new to learn and something new to try. He especially enjoys the excitement of performing live and the personal satisfaction of getting an audience to laugh or cry simply by saying the right words in the right way.

"I dislike pretentious actors and people who take advantage of an actor's desire to perform," he says. "As one of the few professions where there is an abundance of people willing to work for nothing, producers, casting directors, agents, and managers who only care about the money will take advantage of and abuse actors for personal gain. Being an astute actor helps prevent much of this, but one must always be on the lookout."

> Here's another birth-name challenge: Sean Combs.

For More Information

Books

Bekken, Bonnie Bjorguine. *Opportunities in Performing Arts Careers*. McGraw-Hill, 2000.

Bild, Kathryn Marie. *The Actor's Quotation Book: Acting in a Nutshell from Those Who Really Know*. Smith and Kraus, 2003.

Cohen, Robert. *Acting Professionally: Raw Facts About Careers in Acting*. McGraw-Hill, 2003.

Field, Shelly. *Career Opportunities in Theater and the Performing Arts*. Facts on File, 1999.

Ferguson Publishing Staff. *Ferguson's Careers in Focus: Performing Arts*. Ferguson Publishing Company, 2002.

Mauro, Lucia. *Careers for the Stagestruck & Other Dramatic Types*. McGraw-Hill, 2004.

Mitchell, Stephen, and Kathi Carey. *How to Start a Hollywood Career Without Having to Go There: An Instruction Manual for Actors*. Cinebank Productions, 2001.

Pasternak, Ceel, and Linda Thornburg. *Cool Careers for Girls in Performing Arts*. Sagebrush Bound, 2000.

Shepard, John W. *Auditioning and Acting for the Camera: Proven Techniques for Auditioning and Performing in Film, Episodic TV, Sitcoms, Soap Operas, Commercials, and Industrials.* Smith & Kraus, 2004.

Periodicals

Back Stage East
770 Broadway, Fourth Floor
New York, NY 10003
www.backstage.com

Back Stage West
5055 Wilshire Boulevard
Los Angeles, CA 90036
www.backstage.com

Daily Variety Magazine
5700 Wilshire Boulevard, Suite 120
Los Angeles, CA 90036
or
360 Park Avenue South
New York, NY 10010
www.variety.com

Organizations for Actors

Actors' Equity Association
165 West Forty-Sixth Street
New York, NY 10036
www.actorsequity.org

Alliance of Canadian Cinema Television and Radio Artists
625 Church Street
Toronto, ON M4Y 2G1
Canada
www.actra.ca

Alliance of Resident Theatres (A.R.T./New York)
131 Varick Street
New York, NY 10013
www.offbroadwayonline.com

American Alliance for Theatre and Education
7475 Wisconsin Avenue, Suite 300A
Bethesda, MD 20814
www.aate.com

American Association of Community Theatre
8402 Briarwood Circle
Lago Vista, TX 78645
www.aact.org

American Federation of Television and Radio Artists (AFTRA)
New York National Office
260 Madison Avenue
New York, NY 10016
www.aftra.org

American Federation of Television and Radio Artists (AFTRA)
Los Angeles National Office
5757 Wilshire Boulevard, Ninth Floor
Los Angeles, CA 90036
www.aftra.org

American Film Institute
2021 North Western Avenue
Los Angeles, CA 90027
www.afi.com

American Guild of Variety Artists (AGVA)
184 Fifth Avenue, Sixth Floor
New York, NY 10010

American Theatre Works, Inc.
PO Box 510
Dorset, VT 05251
www.dorsettheatrefestival.com

Canadian Actors' Equity Association
44 Victoria Street, Twelfth Floor
Toronto, ON M5C 3C4
Canada
www.caea.com

National Association of Schools of Theatre (NAST)
11250 Roger Bacon Drive, Suite 21
Reston, VA 20190
http://nast.arts-accredit.org

Screen Actors Guild (SAG)
360 Madison Avenue
New York, NY 10017
or
5757 Wilshire Boulevard
Los Angeles, CA 90036
www.sag.org

Theater Communications Group, Inc.
520 Eighth Avenue, Twenty-fourth Floor
New York, NY 10018
www.tcg.org

CHAPTER SEVEN

Musicians

M usic is a basic part of the human experience. On any given day, how long can you go without hearing some type of music?

For some who are class clowns at heart, music is not just something to be heard and enjoyed. Instead, it is an outlet for the desire to perform, whether it takes the form of singing or playing musical instruments.

Are music and performing at the core of your very being, something from which you derive great enjoyment? Has music always been a special part of your life? Have you always longed to appear before audiences? Did you ever stand in front of your mirror and pretend your hairbrush was a microphone? Did you play your musical instruments for friends, family, pets—virtually anyone who would listen? If so, then a career as a musician may be the ideal choice for you.

For Genuine Music Lovers

Successful professional musicians are artists who express themselves through their music by conducting, playing instruments, singing, or all three, at one time or another. Through their talent, many years of hard work, initiative, and perhaps a lucky break, they make a living and entertain audiences doing what they love most—making music.

Some musically inclined individuals succeed early in life. Lorin Maazel conducted two major symphony orchestras before the age of thirteen and went on to enjoy a successful career as an adult conductor. Yehudi Menuhin made his violin debut at age seven. Sergey Prokofiev was already performing as a pianist at the ripe old age of six and composed an opera at the age of nine. His *Peter and the Wolf* has been a source of entertainment for both children and adults for many decades.

No matter how old you are, this chapter will provide you with the information you need to pursue a career in performing music.

Jobs for Musicians

Millions of people play instruments or sing in choirs or amateur groups, but the number of professional musicians is much smaller. About 215,000 men and women are employed as musicians in the United States, according to the U.S. Department of Labor. Included are those who play in regional, metropolitan, or major symphony orchestras. (Large orchestras employ from 85 to 105 musicians, while smaller ones employ 60 to 75 players.) Also counted are those who are a part of hundreds of small orchestras, symphony orchestras, pop and jazz groups, and those who broadcast or record.

Instrumental musicians may play a variety of musical instruments in an orchestra, popular band, marching band, military band, concert band, symphony, dance band, rock group, or jazz group, and their instruments may be string, brass, woodwind, percussion, or electronic synthesizers. A large percentage of musicians are proficient in playing several related instruments, such as the flute and clarinet. Those who are very talented have the option to perform as soloists.

Rehearsing and performing take up much of the musicians' time and energy. In addition, musicians, especially those without agents, may need to perform a number of other routine tasks, such as making travel or rehearsal hall reservations; keeping track of auditions and recording schedules; arranging for amplifiers and other equipment to enhance performances; designing lighting, costuming, and makeup; keeping financial records; and setting up advertising, concerts, tickets, programs, and contracts. In addition, it is necessary for musicians to plan the sequence of the numbers to be performed and/or arrange their music according to the conductor's instructions before performances.

Musicians must also keep their instruments clean, polished, tuned, and in proper working order. In addition, they are expected to attend meetings with agents, employers, and conductors or directors to discuss contracts, engagements, and any other business activities.

Performing musicians encompass a wide variety of careers. Here are just a few of the possibilities.

Section Member

Section members are the individuals who play instruments in an orchestra. They must be talented players and able to learn the music on their own. Rehearsals are strictly designed for putting all of the instruments and individuals together and for establishing cues such as phrasing and correct breathing. It is expected that all musicians practice sufficiently on their own before rehearsals.

Session Musician

The session musician is the one responsible for playing background music in a studio while a recording artist is singing. The session musician may also be called a freelance musician, a backup musician, a session player, or studio musician. Session musicians are used for all kinds of recordings—Broadway musicals, operas, rock and folk songs, and pop tunes.

Versatility is the most important ingredient for these professionals—the more instruments the musician has mastered, the greater number of styles he or she can offer, the more possibilities for musical assignments. Session musicians often are listed through contractors who call upon them when the need arises.

Other possibilities exist through direct requests made by the artists themselves, the group members, or the management team.

The ability to sight-read is important for all musicians, but it is particularly crucial for session musicians. Rehearsal time is usually very limited, and costs make it too expensive to have to do retakes.

Concertmaster

The role of concertmaster is an important one. Those chosen to be concertmasters have the responsibility of leading the string sections of orchestras during both rehearsals and concerts. In addition, these individuals are responsible for tuning the rest of the orchestra. This is the "music" you hear for about fifteen to twenty seconds before the musicians begin to play their first piece.

Concertmasters answer directly to the conductor. They must possess leadership abilities and be very knowledgeable of both the music and all the instruments.

Floor-Show Band Member

Some musicians belong to bands that perform in floor shows and appear in hotels, nightclubs, cruise ships, bars, concert arenas, and cafés. Usually the bands do two shows per night with a particular number of sets in each show. Additionally, they may be required to play one or two dance sets during the course of the engagement. Here, the audience is seated during the shows and gets up to dance during the dance sets. Shows may include costuming, dialogue, singing, jokes, skits, unusual sound effects, and anything else the band decides to include. Floor-show bands may be contracted to appear in one place for one night or several weeks at a time. As expected, a great deal of traveling is involved for those who take up this career.

Choir Director

Choir directors are responsible for recruiting and directing choirs and planning the music programs for churches or temples. They are often given the job of auditioning potential members of the choir, setting up rehearsal schedules, overseeing and directing rehearsals, and choosing the music. They may be in charge of the church's or temple's music library or may designate another individual to oversee it. Working closely with the minister or other religious leader of the congregation, choir directors plan all concerts, programs, and other musical events.

In addition, choir directors develop and maintain the music budgets for their religious institutions. In some cases, choral directors are expected to maintain office hours each week. During those times, they may write music, handle administrative chores, or work with small groups of singers and/or the organist or accompanist.

Usually a bachelor's degree in music is required, with a special emphasis on sacred music. A master's degree may be preferred.

Organist

Organists carry on a long-standing tradition. They play their instruments at religious and special services, such as weddings and funerals. Recitals may also be given as part of the congregation's spiritual programming. Organists choose the music to be played or may work with the choir or music director to accomplish this task. Organists are also responsible for making sure organs are in proper working order and may also advise the congregation on other music-related issues. Sometimes the organist also serves as the choir director or assistant director.

Singer

Singers use their voices as their instrument of choice. Using the techniques of melody, harmony, rhythm, and voice production, they interpret music and both instruct and entertain their audiences. They may sing character parts or perform in their own individual style.

Classical singers are identified by the ranges of their voices: soprano (the highest range), contralto, tenor, baritone, and bass (lowest range). These singers typically perform in operas. Singers of popular music may perform country and western, rap, ethnic, reggae, folk, rock, or jazz as individuals or as part of a group. Often singers also possess the ability to play musical instruments and thus accompany themselves when performing (guitar or piano, for instance).

Religious singers include cantors, soloists, and choir members.

Conductor and Choral Director

The music conductor is the director for all of the performers in a musical presentation, whether they are singing or playing instruments. Although there are many types of conductors—symphony, choral, dance band, opera, marching band, and ballet—in all cases, the music conductor is the one who is in charge of interpreting the music.

Conductors audition and select musicians, choose the music to accommodate the talents and abilities of the musicians, and direct rehearsals and performances, applying conducting techniques to achieve desired musical effects such as harmony, rhythm, tempo, and shading.

Orchestral conductors lead instrumental music groups, such as orchestras, dance bands, and various popular ensembles. Choral directors lead choirs and smaller singing groups, such as glee clubs, sometimes working with a band or orchestra conductor.

Announcer or Disc Jockey

Radio and television announcers play an important role in keeping listeners interested. They are the ones who must read messages, commercials, and scripts in an entertaining, interesting, or enlightening way. They are also responsible for introducing station breaks, and they may interview guests and sell commercial time to advertisers. Sometimes they are called disc jockeys, but actually disc jockeys are the announcers who oversee musical programming.

Disc jockeys must be very knowledgeable about music in general and all aspects of their specialties, specifically the music and the groups who play or sing that kind of music. Their programs may feature general music, rock, pop, country and western, or any specific musical period or style, such as 1960s or 1980s tunes.

Work Settings for Musicians

You'll find musicians working in all kinds of settings. Popular instrumentalists are spread nationwide from small towns to large cities. Many consist of small groups that play at weddings, bar mitzvahs, church events, funerals, school or community concerts, dances, festivals, and other events. Accompanists play for theater productions or dance recitals. Combos, piano or organ soloists, and other musicians play at nightclubs, bars, or restaurants. Musicians may work in opera, musical comedy, and ballet productions or be a part of the armed forces. Well-known musicians and groups give their own concerts, appear live on radio and television programs, make recordings, appear in movies, create music videos, or go on concert tours.

Many musicians work in cities in which there are fairly large populations and where entertainment and recording activities are concentrated, such as Nashville, New York, Los Angeles, San Francisco, Boston, Philadelphia, and Chicago.

Working Conditions for Musicians

The life of a musician is not an easy one. Professional musicians are often forced into work schedules that are long and erratic, depending on how heavy the rehearsal and presentation schedules are. Usually daily practices or rehearsals are required, particularly for new projects. Work weeks in excess of forty hours are common. Travel is often a familiar part of a musician's or singer's life, and a routine that includes daytime, nighttime, weekend, or holiday work is entirely possible.

Musicians who are lucky enough to be hired for a full season (a "master agreement") work for up to fifty-two weeks. Those who must work for more than one employer are always on the lookout for additional gigs, and many supplement their incomes by finding work in other related or unrelated jobs.

Most instrumental musicians come into contact with a variety of other people, including their colleagues, agents, employers, sponsors, and audiences. They usually work indoors, although some may perform outdoors for parades, concerts, and dances. In some taverns and restaurants, smoke and odors may be present, and lighting and ventilation may be inadequate.

Learning the Music Game

Many people who become professional musicians begin studying their instrument of choice (whether it be voice, organ, harp, harpsichord, string, woodwind, brass, or percussion) in childhood and continue the study via private or group lessons throughout elementary and high school. In addition, they usually garner valuable experience by playing in a school or community band or orchestra or with a group of friends.

Singers usually start training when their voices mature. All musicians need extensive and prolonged training to acquire the necessary skills, knowledge, and ability to interpret music. Participation in school musicals, religious institutions, community events, state fairs, bands, or choirs often provides good early training and experience. Necessary formal training may be obtained through conservatory study, college or university study, personal study with a professional, or all of the above.

Over six hundred colleges, universities, and conservatories offer four-year programs that result in a bachelor's degree in music or music education. Usually both pop and classical music are studied. Course work will include classes in music theory, music composition, music interpretation, literature, conducting, drama, foreign languages, acting, and how to play a musical instrument. Other academic studies include course work in science, literature, philosophy, and the arts. Classroom instruction, reading assignments, discussion groups, and actual performances are included. A large number of performances are encouraged and expected, and students are evaluated on their progress during their time at the college.

At the undergraduate level, a typical program for a violin major might consist of the following courses:

- Instrument
- Materials and Literature
- Ear Training
- Piano
- Music History
- Orchestra
- Piano and Strings Chamber Music
- String Quartet
- Introduction to Literature
- French, German, Italian, or Spanish (or another foreign language)
- Academic electives

The types of schools offering such courses vary widely. Here is an example of several.

Small College

Brenau University, a small college in Gainesville, Georgia, offers a bachelor's degree program in performance. Areas of concentration include voice, piano, and piano accompanying.

The advantages of this type of school are that classes tend to be small, the atmosphere is friendly, and students receive a great deal of one-on-one attention. Before they can major in music, Brenau students must go through an audition. Once accepted, they complete courses such as the following:

- History of Music
- Theory
- History
- Period History
- Choir
- Major Instrument
- Minor Instrument
- Conducting
- Diction
- Opera Literature
- Music Literature and Pedagogy

They also complete electives in music, theater, dance, or foreign languages, along with general education courses in English, math and other areas. For more information, contact:

Director of Music
Brenau University
One Centennial Circle
Gainesville, GA 30501
www.brenau.edu

Large University

At a large university, students generally have access to more programs than at smaller schools, including those at the graduate level. In addition, more courses within each program may also be available.

Michigan State University, for instance, offers a bachelor of music degree in music performance with concentrations in five performance areas: piano, stringed instruments, wind instruments, percussion instruments, or voice. A piano pedagogy option is also available.

Piano majors, for example, must take the following courses in addition to meeting performance requirements and completing general education courses:

- Chamber Music
- Keyboard Skills
- Conducting for Music Performance Majors
- Keyboard Methods and Literature
- Piano Accompanying
- Piano Performance
- Keyboard Literature to Mid-Nineteenth Century
- Keyboard Literature since the Mid-Nineteenth Century

They also must complete two of these courses:

- History of Oratorio
- Song Literature: German
- Art Song Literature: European and American
- Music of the Eighteenth Century
- Nineteenth-Century European and American Music Literature
- Twentieth-Century European and American Music Literature
- History of Opera

Students in other areas have a similarly diverse range of course selections.

Community College

For students who don't want to spend four years or more in college, or who would like to save money and transfer later, community college programs can be ideal if music courses are available.

At Lewis and Clark Community College in Illinois, students may earn an associate in fine arts degree in music performance. Programs are also available in music business, music theory, jazz studies, jazz performance, theory and composition, sacred music, and music pedagogy.

Along with general education requirements, students complete courses such as Music Theory, Music Literature and History, Introduction to Music Literature, and hands-on instruction with the instruments of their choice, including trombone, tuba, percussion, violin, string bass, electric bass, guitar, piano, organ, or voice.

Basic Traits for Success

Those who are considering careers in music definitely need musical talent. They also should have improvisational skills, versatility, the ability to sight-read, outstanding music memory, finger dexterity, the ability to distinguish differences in pitch, determination, imagination, creativity, perseverance, the ability to work with others, poise, and stage presence.

Since high-quality performance requires constant study and practice, self-discipline is vital. Moreover, musicians who play concert and nightclub engagements must have physical stamina because frequent travel and night performances are required. They must also be prepared to face the anxiety of intermittent employment and rejections when auditioning for work.

For announcers and disc jockeys, additional education beyond secondary school, particularly course work in areas such as public speaking, writing, English, communications, music, or radio and television broadcasting, is very advantageous. Desirable personal qualities include charisma, a pleasing voice, a good sense of humor, and expertise about the field of music. In addition, gaining experience as a production assistant or writer is beneficial, as well as securing a radio telephone operator permit from the Federal Communications Commission (FCC).

Musical conductors must have at least a high school diploma (and usually a college education) and knowledge of the arts, musical history, harmony, and theory. Some understanding of languages, such as French, German, Latin, and Italian, can also be helpful. Desirable qualities include charisma, a great ear for music, an air of style, and both business and musical savvy. Also desirable are knowledge of a wide range of instruments, advanced sight-reading skills, a sense of showmanship, the ability to lead, skills in performing in an appealing way, and the ability to use a baton to control timing, rhythm, and structure. Individuals become musical conductors only after spending many years as musicians while studying to become conductors.

Earnings for Musicians

The range of financial rewards for musicians is wide. According to the U.S. Department of Labor, median annual earnings of salaried musicians and singers were just over $36,000 in 2002. The middle 50 percent earned between $18,660 and $59,970. While the lowest 10 percent earned less than $13,040, the highest 10 percent earned more than $96,250. Salaries tended to be higher than average in performing arts companies and lower in religious organizations.

For a relative few who become famous, earnings may be in the millions of dollars annually. This is not true just of rock stars; some orchestra conductors earn seven-figure salaries. But for most performers, such earnings will never be a realistic possibility.

A number of factors may affect income. Earnings often depend on the number of hours and weeks worked per year, a performer's professional reputation, and the setting. The most successful musicians earn performance or recording fees that far exceed the median earnings.

The American Federation of Musicians has reported that weekly minimum salaries in major orchestras ranged from $734 to $1,925 during the 2002–2003 performing season. Each orchestra works out a separate contract with its local union, and individual musicians are eligible to negotiate salary variations. While top orchestras have a season ranging from twenty-four to fifty-two weeks, regional orchestras tend to have fewer performances. As a result, minimum salaries are often lower. The same is true in community orchestras, which often have even more limited levels of funding.

Some musicians employed by larger symphony orchestras work under master wage agreements that guarantee a season's work up to fifty-two weeks. Other musicians, however, may face relatively long periods of unemployment between jobs. Even when employed, it is very common for musicians and singers to work part-time in unrelated occupations. Because they may not work steadily for one employer, some performers cannot qualify for unemployment compensation, and few have typical benefits such as sick leave or paid vacations. As a result, many musicians give private lessons or take jobs unrelated to music to supplement their earnings as performers.

Many musicians belong to a local of the American Federation of Musicians. Professional singers usually belong to a branch of the Associated Actors and Artists of America.

Future Prospects for Musicians

Music is a crowded field. Competition for musician jobs is keen, and talent alone is no guarantee of success. The glamour and potential high earnings in this occupation attracts many talented and ambitious individuals.

The U.S. Department of Labor projects that overall employment of musicians will grow about as fast as the average for all occupations through the year 2012. Most new wage and salary jobs for musicians will be found in religious organizations and in bands, orchestras, and other entertainment groups. Slower-than-average growth is projected for self-employed musicians, such as those who perform in nightclubs, restaurants, concert tours, and elsewhere.

Competition is always great for announcers or disc jockeys. They must sometimes work on a freelance rather than a salaried basis. Ongoing changes in the world of radio, such as the growth of syndicated programs and the rise of satellite radio, may limit the number of openings in the future.

For musical conductors, the outlook is not especially promising. Job openings will be limited, and competition to fill them will be fierce.

Career Development Strategies in Music

The Job Search

In a way, getting ready for a job search is like getting ready to do battle; you must arm yourself with all the best weapons available to you and make the best possible plan of attack. The best weapons available to you include a well-designed resume, a well-conceived cover letter, a well-selected portfolio, and an audition tape or disc in the form of video or audio.

The Resume

For prospective musicians or for those who aspire to other performing careers, a resume is an essential tool just as it is for other career fields. A resume should include significant information that would make an employer want to hire you above all others, or at the least grant you an interview. Standing as a summary of your experience, skills and abilities, strengths, accomplishments, and education, the resume's importance cannot be underestimated.

Most experts agree that the best approach is to keep a resume focused and as brief as possible. Complete sentences are not necessary; phrases are acceptable.

Keep your resume to a maximum of two pages—one is even better. Don't list everything you ever did in your life; highlight important skills and accomplishments.

One type of resume, the chronological resume, includes the following elements:

Heading. Provide a heading at the top of the page that includes your name, home address, e-mail address, and phone number(s). Invest in an answering machine or answering service if you don't already have one—it's an absolute necessity!

Work Experience. This will be the main part of your resume, where your prospective employers will focus to determine whether or not you have the right qualifications for the job. So here is where you must show your expertise by emphasizing your accomplishments. Work experience is usually listed in reverse chronological order, beginning with your most recent position. Entries should be complete, listing the job title, dates of employment, employer, and location, as well as descriptions of your responsibilities in each position. Use action verbs. Passive words don't have the same impact.

Education. Next to work experience, education is most important. Include all of the schools you've attended, the degrees you've earned, your field of concentration, and relevant extracurricular activities (student choral director, for example).

Other Elements. In addition, your resume might include the following sections:

- Professional Associations
- Awards and Honors
- Special Skills
- References

Nowadays, many resumes are posted online rather than printed and mailed or hand delivered, but the same basic principles still apply.

The Cover Letter

A cover letter is a document that sells the recipient on reading the resume. Cover letters are not used as frequently as they once were, since so many job applications are now submitted electronically. But they still have their place when resumes are mailed to potential employers, and electronic versions can also be helpful.

When used, a cover letter should be directed to a specific person whose name and spelling you have verified. Cover letters should be tailored to each specific company or job opening. Don't use a form letter here, although some of the information, including the job you are seeking and some elements of your professional background, may be the same.

Cover letters should consist of the following elements:

1. A salutation directed specifically to the person who can hire you.
2. The opening, something that catches the attention of the reader. Be creative! Introduce yourself and specify the job for which you want to be considered. If you have a referral name, by all means mention it, and if you are responding to an ad, state that. If possible, show your researching skills by pointing out something new or positive you know about this employment possibility.
3. The body provides a brief summary of your qualifications for the job and refers to the resume, which will reinforce your selling campaign to win an interview or audition.
4. In the closing, request an interview and state your intention to follow up with a call, preferably on a specific date. If to be printed rather than submitted electronically, use the standard closing, "Sincerely yours," and type your name, leaving room in between for you to sign your name. It's not a bad idea to put your address, phone number, and e-mail address under your name in the event your letter gets separated from the resume, which includes that vital information.

Avenues to Music-Related Jobs

What path leads to a job in music? The possibilities are wide ranging. Those who study music at an educational institution may find their first jobs by going through the school's career-services office. Working closely with these human-resource professionals can provide you with a wealth of worthwhile advice. For example, since orchestra musicians usually audition for positions after completing their formal training, career-services staff at your school may provide you with a list of possible audition locations.

Finding positions through want ads or ads published in trade journals is still a popular form of seeking jobs. Even more common nowadays is the use of Internet job sites and those maintained by employers. Professional organizations and associations may also offer you direct employment possibilities or provide you with agencies, companies, or other employers or contacts that may eventually evolve into positions. Consider joining an association that caters to your own musical specialty or to the field of music in general.

It is important to realize that, no matter what the field, the majority of people find their jobs through networking. That means that you must make a concerted effort to let people know what your expertise is and that you are available. Talk to friends and acquaintances; go to club meetings and association workshops. Volunteer to help with an event. Converse with people you deal with in everyday life: cleaners, bank tellers, personal accountants—anyone you can think of. Of course, you may not hear about an opening directly, but one person may give you the name of another to contact, which could eventually lead to a job. In the music business, it is wise to get to know as many people as possible, not only to make contacts that will lead to jobs, but in order to make contacts that may lead to internships, volunteer opportunities, or part-time work.

Send a resume and cover letter to everyone you know who has any link to the music business. Let people know whether you have a tape or CD available that showcases your performing ability. If they want to hear it, they'll get back in touch (don't send these things out if they are not requested). Keep track of the responses, and follow up with people who respond.

Individual musicians often join together with others to form local bands. Once a group is formed, you can advertise by placing ads, putting up notices, and spreading the message by word of mouth. You might also want to create a website for the band. After building a reputation, you may be able to obtain work through a booking agent or be qualified to become part of larger, more established groups.

After having some performing under your belt, you might visit recording studios and talk to anyone you can. Tell them about yourself, your experience, your musical specialties. Make sure you leave your business card (or a sheet with your contact information and experience listed) with your instrument written on it. In fact, always carry cards with you and pass them out whenever you possibly can. You may need to have a demo CD made to leave with possible employers. Demos, which are recordings of your voice or instrumental work, provide a good way to display your talents at their very best.

Here's a final birth-name challenge: Ramon Estevez.

For More Information

Periodicals
Billboard
1515 Broadway
New York, NY 10036
www.billboard.com

Canadian Musician
23 Hanover Drive
St. Catharine's, ON L2W 1A3
Canada
www.canadianmusician.com

Books

Avalon, Moses. *Confessions of a Record Producer: How to Survive the Scams and Shams of the Music Business.* Backbeat Books, 2002.

Avalon, Moses. *Secrets of Negotiating a Record Contract: The Musician's Guide to Understanding and Avoiding Sneaky Lawyer Tricks.* Backbeat Books, 2001.

Baker, Bob. *Guerrilla Music Marketing Handbook: 201 Self-Promotion Ideas for Songwriters, Musicians & Bands.* Spotlight Publications, 2001.

Brabec, Jeffrey, and Todd Brabec. *Music, Money, and Success: The Insider's Guide to Making Money in the Music Business.* Schirmer Trade Books, 2002.

Davis, Richard. *Becoming an Orchestral Musician: A Guide for Aspiring Professionals.* Giles de La Mare, 2004.

Field, Shelly. *Career Opportunities in the Music Industry.* Facts on File, 2000.

Goldberg, Jan; Stephen E. Lambert; and Julie Degalan. *Great Jobs for Music Majors.* McGraw-Hill, 1998.

Hatschek, Keith; Kristen Schilo; and Susan Gedutis. *How to Get a Job in the Music and Recording Industry.* Berklee Press Publications, 2001.

Johnson, Jeff. *Careers for Music Lovers & Other Tuneful Types.* McGraw-Hill, 2003.

Kalmar, Veronika. *Label Launch: A Guide to Independent Record Recording, Promotion, and Distribution.* St. Martin's Press, 2002.

Krasilovsky, M. William; Sidney Shemel; and John M. Gross. *This Business of Music: The Definitive Guide to the Music Industry.* Billboard Books, 2003.

Des Pres, Josquin, and Mark Landsman. *Creative Careers in Music*. Allworth Press, 2004.
Spellman, Peter. *The Self-Promoting Musician: Strategies for Independent Music Success*. Berklee Press Publications, 1999.
Thall, Peter M. *What They'll Never Tell You About the Music Business: The Myths, Secrets, Lies (& a Few Truths)*. Watson-Guptill Publications, 2002.

Organizations

There are literally hundreds of professional associations that provide benefits to members. Here are some of them.

Academy of Country Music (ACM)
4100 West Alameda Avenue, Suite 208
Burbank, CA 91505
www.acmcountry.com

American Choral Directors Association (ACDA)
545 Couch Drive
Oklahoma City, OK 73102
www.acdaonline.org

American Federation of Musicians (AFM)
1501 Broadway, Suite 600
New York, NY 10036
www.afm.org

AFM Canadian Office
75 The Donway West, Suite 1010
Don Mills, ON M3C 2E9
Canada
www.afm.org

American Federation of Television and Radio Artists (AFTRA)
New York National Office
260 Madison Avenue
New York, NY 10016
or
Los Angeles National Office
5757 Wilshire Boulevard, Ninth Floor
Los Angeles, CA 90036
www.aftra.org

American Guild of Music (AGM)
PO Box 599
Warren, MI 48090
www.americanguild.org

American Guild of Musical Artists (AGMA)
1430 Broadway, Fourteenth Floor
New York, NY 10018
www.musicalartists.org

American Guild of Organists (AGO)
475 Riverside Drive, Suite 1260
New York, NY 10115
www.agohq.org

American Music Conference (AMC)
5790 Armada Drive
Carlsbad, CA 92008
www.amc-music.org

American Musicological Society (AMS)
201 South Thirty-fourth Street
Philadelphia, PA 19104
www.sas.upenn.edu/music/ams

American Symphony Orchestra League (ASOL)
910 Seventeenth Street NW
Washington, DC 20006
or
33 West Sixtieth Street, Fifth Floor
New York, NY 10023
www.symphony.org

Broadcast Music, Inc. (BMI)
320 West Fifty-seventh Street
New York, NY 10019
www.bmi.com

Canadian Academy of Recording Arts and Sciences (CARAS)
355 King Street West, Suite 501
Toronto, ON M5V 1J6
Canada
www.carasonline.ca

Canadian Country Music Association
5 Director Court, Unit 102
Woodbridge, ON L46 4S5
Canada
www.ccma.org

Canadian League of Composers
Canadian Music Center
20 Saint Joseph Street
Toronto, ON M4Y 1J9
Canada
www.composition.org

Chamber Music America
305 Seventh Avenue, Fifth Floor
New York, NY 10001
www.chamber-music.org

Chorus America
1156 Fifteenth Street NW, Suite 310
Washington, DC 20005
www.chorusamerica.org

College Music Society
312 East Pine Street
Missoula, MT 59802
www.music.org

Concert Artists Guild (CAG)
850 Seventh Avenue, Suite 1205
New York, NY 10019
www.concertartists.org

Country Music Association (CMA)
One Music Circle South
Nashville, TN 37203
www.countrymusic.org

Gospel Music Association (GMA)
1205 Division Street
Nashville, TN 37203
www.gospelmusic.org

International Conference of Symphony and Opera Musicians
  (ICSOM)
6607 Waterman
St. Louis, MO 63130
www.icsom.org

Metropolitan Opera Association (MOA)
Lincoln Center
New York NY 10023
www.metopera.org

Music Critics Association of North America
722 Dulaney Valley Road, #259
Baltimore, MD 21204
www.mcana.org

National Academy of Popular Music (NAPM)
330 West Fifty-eighth, Suite 411
New York, NY 10019
www.songwritershalloffame.org

National Academy of Recording Arts and Sciences (NARAS)
The Recording Academy
3402 Pico Boulevard
Santa Monica, CA 90405
www.grammy.com

National Association of Schools of Music
11250 Roger Bacon Drive, Suite 21
Reston, VA 20190
http://nasm.arts-accredit.org

National Association of Teachers of Singing
4745 Sutton Park, Suite 201
Jacksonville, FL 32224
www.nats.org

National Orchestral Association (NOA)
PO Box 7016
New York, NY 10150
www.nationalorchestral.org

National Opera Association
PO Box 60869
Canyon, TX 79016
www.noa.org

National Youth Orchestra of Canada
258 Adelaide Street East, Suite 400
Toronto, ON M5A 1N1
Canada
www.nyoc.org

Opera America
1156 Fifteenth Street NW, Suite 810
Washington, DC 20005
www.operaamerica.org

Orchestras Canada
56 The Esplanade, Suite 203
Toronto, ON M5E 1A7
Canada
www.oc.ca

Society of Professional Audio Recording Studios
9 Music Square South, Suite 222
Nashville, TN 37203
www.spars.com

Songwriters Association of Canada
26 Soho Street, Suite 340
Toronto, ON M5T 2S2
Canada
www.songwriters.ca

Songwriters Guild of America
1500 Harbor Boulevard
Weehawkin, NJ 07086
www.songwriters.org

Songwriters Hall of Fame
330 West Fifty-eighth Street, Suite 411
New York, NY 10019
www.songwritershalloffame.org

Women in Music National Network
31121 Mission Boulevard, Suite 300
Hayward, CA 94544
www.womeninmusic.com

Name Quiz Answers

Chapter One: David Adkins is comedian Sinbad.

Chapter Two: Marshall Mathers III is singer Eminem.

Chapter Three: Dwayne Johnson is actor The Rock.

Chapter Four: Terry Jean Bollette is wrestler and actor Hulk Hogan.

Chapter Five: Jennifer Anastassakis is actress Jennifer Aniston.

Chapter Six: Sean Combs is rapper P. Diddy (formerly Puff Daddy).

Chapter Seven: Ramon Estevez is actor Martin Sheen.

About the Author

Jan Goldberg's love for the printed page began well before her second birthday. Regular visits to the book bindery where her grandfather worked produced a magic combination of sights and smells that she carries with her to this day.

Childhood was filled with composing poems and stories, reading books, and playing library. Elementary and high school included an assortment of contributions to school newspapers. While a full-time college student, Goldberg wrote extensively as part of her job responsibilities in the College of Business Administration at Roosevelt University in Chicago. After receiving a degree in elementary education, she was able to extend her love of reading and writing to her students.

Goldberg has written extensively in the occupations area for *Career World Magazine,* as well as for the many career publications produced by CASS Recruitment Publications. She has also contributed to a number of projects for educational publishers, including Scott Foresman and Addison-Wesley.

As a feature writer, Goldberg's work has appeared in *Parenting, Today's Chicago Woman, Opportunity Magazine, Chicago Parent, Complete Woman Magazine, North Shore Magazine,* and Pioneer Press newspapers. In all, she has published more than 250 pieces as a full-time freelance writer.

In addition to *Careers for Class Clowns,* other books she has written for McGraw-Hill include: *Careers for Color Connoisseurs, Great Jobs for Music Majors, Careers in Journalism,* and *Opportunities in Research and Development Careers.*